# Marriage

## A Fortress for Well-Being

# Marriage

## A Fortress for Well-Being

BAHÁ'Í PUBLISHING
WILMETTE, ILLINOIS

Bahá'í Publishing
401 Greenleaf Avenue, Wilmette, Illinois 60091-2844

 Published 2009
Printed in the United States of America
on acid-free paper ∞

25 24 23 22 9 8 7 6

Library of Congress Cataloging-in-Publication Data
Marriage : a fortress for well-being. —Rev. ed.
p. cm.
Includes bibliographical references and index.
ISBN 978-1-931847-63-6 (pbk. : alk. paper)
1. Marriage—Religious aspects—Bahai Faith.
HQ525.B33F67 2009
297.9'3563—dc22
2009023040

Cover design by Bob Reddy
Book design by Patrick Falso

# Table of Contents

**Part Two: Preparation for Marriage in Light of God's Purpose for Humanity**

# Foreword

What is marriage? In the Bahá'í Faith, marriage is described as a "fortress for well-being," a divine institution that improves the spiritual life of the marriage partners and fosters the spiritual and social development of their children. Marriage itself is fundamental to the growth of an ever-advancing civilization. The Bahá'í writings state that with the coming of each new Prophet or Manifestation of God and the inauguration of each new cycle in religious history, some social laws are abrogated, but the law of marriage remains eternal.

*Foreword*

The world's great religious traditions have recognized the fundamental human and social need to marry, and they have placed great sacred meaning on the act. In the scriptures of the Abrahamic religions—Judaism, Christianity, and Islam—one finds extensive laws related to marriage and family life. In many religious traditions marriage is seen as a covenant blessed by and accountable to God. Marriage is the means by which the next generation is raised up to know and serve God; it is how children are protected, and it is how the stability and advancement of civilization are ensured.

The Bahá'í writings on marriage are especially relevant to our era. Today, all around us, we witness a collapsing world order and family life too often reflects this chaos and despair. In the United States today, 43 percent of first marriages end in divorce.[1] The national out-of-wedlock birth rate is now 40 percent and far higher in some communities.[2] Too many children lack the presence of at least one of their parents—often their father—in their daily lives, or they must travel between two homes to stay in touch with both parents.

These losses have lasting consequences. A large body of studies now shows that children raised outside of intact marriages are significantly more likely

---

1. About 43 percent of first marriages will end in divorce in the first fifteen years. Bramlett, Matthew and William Mosher. "First marriage dissolution, divorce, and remarriage: United States," *Advance Data from Vital and Health Statistics* 323. Hyattsville, MD: National Center for Health Statistics: 21.

2. National Center for Health Statistics, 2007.

than other children to use drugs, to drop out of school, to commit crimes, to suffer from depression and emotional distress, to be neglected or abused, to be sexually active early, to commit or consider suicide, and later in life to get divorced themselves and to bear children outside of marriage. These findings are prevalent even in studies that take into consideration the impact of income and other relevant variables that might also cause such outcomes.[3]

Today, even young people raised in successful families fear that the odds of failure in their own marriages are high. And those raised with an absent parent long to prevent such pain for their

---

3. See *Why Marriage Matters: 26 Conclusions from the Social Sciences, 2nd edition* (New York: Institute for American Values, 2005).

own children. Thus the common hope young people today share as they approach marriage is *unity.* They hope to build strong, unified families that can withstand the challenges of twenty-first century life. They hope to raise whole, happy children who will contribute positively to their society, children who will grow up to form their own loving marriages and raise up the next generation. Fortunately, the Bahá'í writings have much to offer on the subject.

Bahá'í marriage creates a "fortress for well-being" for the marriage partners and their children. When the wife and husband seek together to know and to serve God—by recognizing the Manifestation of God for the day in which we live and by following His laws—they acquire the freedom to support one another lovingly, helping one another to develop virtues and to grow spiritually. Such a union provides an ideal environment for the social and spiritual development of their children.

'Abdu'l-Bahá—the son and appointed successor of Bahá'u'lláh, the Prophet and Founder of the Bahá'í Faith—states "there are imperfections in every human being, and you will always become unhappy if you look toward the people themselves."[4] He counseled that we should instead look to the love of God as the true source of love for one another. Then, "Each sees in the other the Beauty of God reflected in the soul, and finding this point of similarity, they are attracted to one another in love. . . .

4. *The Promulgation of Universal Peace*, p. 128.

This love will bring the realization of true accord, the foundation of real unity."[5]

The Bahá'í writings offer a perspective on marriage that is at times radically different from the model of relationships found in society today. Bahá'í standards imply that in determining a suitable marriage partner, it may be wise to avoid typical dating practices, which do not allow someone to really get to know another person, and instead engage in some form of work or service together. A person's maturity and character are revealed in the face of tests or struggles that can arise in such settings. According to Bahá'í law, a couple wishing to get married must seek consent from all their living, natural parents.

---

5. *Paris Talks*, no. 58.7.

This requirement seeks to promote unity and to protect and support the newly formed family. When marriages face routine problems or serious challenges, the tool of consultation can be used to air concerns and make decisions that promote, rather than harm, family unity. The Bahá'í Faith strongly discourages divorce and counsels partners seeking divorce to undertake a "year of patience," during which time they should seek help and make all possible efforts to reconcile.

The sacred writings found in this book provide profound insight and practical advice on a wide range of issues related to the preparation for and the sustaining of a healthy marriage. They empower couples to build families in which "the injury of one shall be considered the injury of all; the comfort of each, the comfort of all; the honor of one, the honor of all."[6] It is hoped that the next generation of married couples and parents will find a great deal of encouragement in the pages that follow.

—Elizabeth Marquardt

---

6. *The Promulgation of Universal Peace*, p. 233.

# Part I

# UNDERSTANDING MARRIAGE IN LIGHT OF GOD'S PURPOSE FOR HUMANITY

— 1 —

# God's Purpose for Humanity: Implications for Marriage

Important determinants of the success of a marriage are the convictions of the couple concerning the purpose of life and its fulfillment. A couple's commitment to and their expectations of each other are often based on this shared understanding of the purpose of life. These commitments and expectations will, in turn, affect their feelings and behavior toward each other, thereby determining the quality of their relationship. This is true of human relationships in general, but it has particular significance for the marital relationship because of its extensive implications for the stability of the family and society.

Bahá'í marriage can best be understood in light of the Bahá'í teachings on God's purpose for humanity. Our primary purpose is to recognize the Manifestation of God for the day in which we live and to follow His laws. When a husband and wife make their marriage serve God's purpose for humanity, it will be based on the spiritual reality of humanity and will therefore become a "fortress for well-being."* As a divine institution, it will also provide

* Bahá'u'lláh, in Bahá'u'lláh, the Báb, and 'Abdu'l-Bahá, *Bahá'í Prayers,* p. 118.

all the essentials for fostering the spiritual and social development of children. Thus, gaining a fuller understanding of God's purpose for humanity is the best preparation for marriage and the most effective preserver of a marital union that has already been formed.

> *The first duty prescribed by God for His servants is the recognition of Him Who is the Dayspring of His Revelation and the Fountain of His laws, Who representeth the Godhead in both the Kingdom of His Cause and the world of creation. Whoso achieveth this duty hath attained unto all good. . . .* —Bahá'u'lláh
>
> (The Kitáb-i-Aqdas, ¶1)

> *The purpose underlying all creation is the revelation of this most sublime, this most holy Day, the Day known*

*as the Day of God, in His Books and Scriptures. . . .* —Bahá'u'lláh

(Quoted in *The Advent of Divine Justice*, ¶110)

*The purpose of God in creating man hath been, and will ever be, to enable him to know his Creator and to attain His Presence.*—Bahá'u'lláh

(*Gleanings from the Writings of Bahá'u'lláh*, no. 29.1)

*I bear witness, O my God, that Thou hast created me to know Thee and to worship Thee.*—Bahá'u'lláh

(*Bahá'í Prayers*, p. 4)

*Having created the world and all that liveth and moveth therein, He, through the direct operation of His unconstrained and sovereign Will, chose to confer upon man the unique distinction and capacity to know Him and to love Him—a capacity that must needs be regarded as the generating impulse and the primary purpose underlying the whole of creation.*—Bahá'u'lláh

(*Gleanings from the Writings of Bahá'u'lláh*, no. 27.2)

*All men have been created to carry forward an ever-advancing civilization. The Almighty beareth Me witness: To act like the beasts of the field is unworthy of man. Those virtues that befit his dignity are forbearance, mercy, compassion and loving-kindness towards all the peoples and kindreds of the earth.*—Bahá'u'lláh

(*Gleanings from the Writings of Bahá'u'lláh*, no. 109.2)

(The purpose of our lives is) *to acquire virtues.*—'Abdu'l-Bahá
(*Paris Talks*, no. 55.2)

*Of the principles enshrined in these Tablets the most vital of them all is the principle of the oneness and wholeness of the human race, which may well be regarded as the hallmark of Bahá'u'lláh's Revelation and the pivot of His teachings. Of such cardinal importance is this principle of unity that it is expressly referred to in the Book of His Covenant, and He unreservedly proclaims it as the central purpose of His Faith.*
—Shoghi Effendi
(*God Passes By*, pp. 216–17)

Because our spiritual progress and fulfillment depend upon an awareness and an acceptance of our purpose in life, the ideal conditions for marriage are those that assist men and women to know and love God and His creation, to acquire virtues, to promote the oneness of mankind,* and to carry forward an ever-advancing civilization. When partners in marriage strive mutually to foster these aspirations in each other, sacrifice of self is required. When this is achieved they will find, in the words of 'Abdu'l-Bahá, *"ideal relationship, union and happiness."*† When marriage partners are united, they are happier, more

* Rúḥíyyih Rabbani has reported ("To the Bahá'í Youth," p. 6) that Shoghi Effendi said "the object of life to a Bahá'í is to promote the oneness of mankind." See also Shoghi Effendi, *The World Order of Bahá'u'lláh,* pp. 43–44.

† 'Abdu'l-Bahá, in *Bahá'í World Faith,* p. 373.

effective in their service to others, and freer to develop spiritually, morally, and intellectually.

## CARRYING FORWARD AN EVER-ADVANCING CIVILIZATION

Marriage is the foundation of a good family; good families in turn are the foundation of a stable civilization. Spiritual marriages will produce spiritual families, from which a spiritual civilization may emerge.

*O peerless Lord! In Thine almighty wisdom Thou hast enjoined marriage upon the peoples, that the generations of men may succeed one another in this contingent world, and that ever, so long as the world shall last, they may busy themselves at the Threshold of Thy oneness*

*with servitude and worship, with salutation, adoration and praise.*
—'Abdu'l-Bahá

(*Bahá'í Prayers*, pp. 118–19)

*Compare the nations of the world to the members of a family. A family is a nation in miniature. Simply enlarge the circle of the household, and you have the nation. Enlarge the circle of nations, and you have all humanity. The conditions surrounding the family surround the nation. The happenings in the family are the happenings in the life of the nation. Would it add to the progress and advancement of a family if dissensions should arise among its members, all fighting, pillaging each other, jealous and revengeful of injury, seeking selfish advantage? Nay, this would be*

*the cause of the effacement of progress and advancement. So it is in the great family of nations, for nations are but an aggregate of families.*
—'Abdu'l-Bahá

(*The Promulgation of Universal Peace*, p. 217)

*According to the teachings of Bahá'u'lláh the family, being a human unit, must be educated according to the rules of sanctity. All the virtues must be taught the family. The integrity of the family bond must be constantly considered, and the rights of the individual members must not be transgressed. . . . The unity of the family must be sustained. The injury of one shall be considered the injury of all; the*

> *comfort of each, the comfort of all; the honor of one, the honor of all.*
> —'Abdu'l-Bahá
>
> (*The Promulgation of Universal Peace*, pp. 232–33)

Because they do not contribute to the progress of civilization in this day, Bahá'u'lláh forbids monastic celibacy and ascetic practices:

> *In this Day, however, let them* [monks and priests] *give up the life of seclusion and direct their steps towards the open world and busy themselves with that which will profit themselves and others. We have granted them leave to enter into wedlock that they may bring forth one who will make mention of God,*

*the Lord of the seen and the unseen, the Lord of the Exalted Throne.*
—Bahá'u'lláh

(*Tablets of Bahá'u'lláh*, p. 24)

*O people of the earth! Living in seclusion or practicing asceticism is not acceptable in the presence of God. It behoveth them that are endued with insight and understanding to observe that which will cause joy and radiance. . . . Deprive not yourselves of the bounties which have been created for your sake.*
—Bahá'u'lláh

(*Tablets of Bahá'u'lláh*, p. 71)

*It must not be implied that one should give up avocation and attainment to livelihood. On the contrary, in the*

*Cause of Bahá'u'lláh monasticism and asceticism are not sanctioned. In this great Cause the light of guidance is shining and radiant. Bahá'u'lláh has even said that occupation and labor are devotion. All humanity must obtain a livelihood by sweat of the brow and bodily exertion, at the same time seeking to lift the burden of others, striving to be the source of comfort to souls and facilitating the means of living. This in itself is devotion to God. Bahá'u'lláh has thereby encouraged action and stimulated service. But the energies of the heart must not be attached to these things; the soul must not be completely occupied with them. Though the mind is busy, the heart must be attracted toward the Kingdom of God in order that the virtues of humanity may be attained from every direction and source.*—'Abdu'l-Bahá

(*The Promulgation of Universal Peace*, pp. 260–61)

## PROMOTING THE ONENESS OF MANKIND

Oneness and unity depend upon freedom from prejudice and upon trust and love. Children learn how to trust and love from the experiences they have with their parents and members of the Bahá'í community. If the relationship between parents is characterized by love and trust, and if the home and community are free from prejudice, the children will be free from prejudice.

*May you become as the waves of one sea, stars of the same heaven, fruits*

*adorning the same tree, roses of one garden in order that through you the oneness of humanity may establish its temple in the world of mankind, for you are the ones who are called to uplift the cause of unity among the nations of the earth.* —'Abdu'l-Bahá

(*The Promulgation of Universal Peace*, pp. 299–300)

*Bahá'u'lláh spent His life teaching this lesson of Love and Unity. Let us then put away from us all prejudice and intolerance, and strive with all our hearts and souls to bring about understanding and unity.* . . . —'Abdu'l-Bahá

(*Paris Talks*, no. 13.20)

*The most important principle of divine philosophy is the oneness of*

*the world of humanity, the unity of mankind, the bond conjoining East and West, the tie of love which blends human hearts.*

*Therefore, it is our duty to put forth our greatest efforts and summon all our energies in order that the bonds of unity and accord may be established among mankind.* —'Abdu'l-Bahá

(*The Promulgation of Universal Peace*, pp. 42–43)

*Wherever a Bahá'í community exists, whether large or small, let it be distinguished for its abiding sense of security and faith, its high standard of rectitude, its complete freedom from all forms of prejudice, the spirit*

*of love among its members, and for the close knit fabric of its social life.*
—The Universal House of Justice
(*Messages from the Universal House of Justice, 1963–1986*, p. 12)

*Bahá'u'lláh tells us that prejudice in its various forms destroys the edifice of humanity. We are adjured by the Divine Messenger to eliminate all forms of prejudices from our lives. Our outer lives must show forth our beliefs. The world must see that, regardless of each passing whim or current fashion of the generality of mankind the Bahá'í lives his life according to the tenets of his Faith. We must not allow the fear of rejection by our friends and neighbours to deter us from our goal to live the*

*Bahá'í life. Let us strive to blot out from lives every last trace of prejudice—racial, religious, political, economic, national, tribal, class, cultural, and that which is based on differences of education or age. We shall be distinguished . . . if our lives are adorned with this principle.*
—The Universal House of Justice
(*Lights of Guidance*, no. 1795)

Oneness does not mean sameness; it means unity in diversity.* In the Bahá'í community, it is common to find marriages between persons of different racial, linguistic, national, and cultural heritages. They draw their respective families into wider circles of unity and create new families that will grow and

* Shoghi Effendi, *World Order of Bahá'u'lláh*, pp. 42–45.

develop in accordance with the principle of the oneness of mankind.

> *Consider the flowers of a garden. Though differing in kind, color, form and shape, yet . . . this diversity increaseth their charm and addeth unto their beauty. How unpleasing to the eye if all the flowers and plants, the leaves and blossoms, the fruit, the branches and the trees of that garden were all of the same shape and color! Diversity of hues, form and shape enricheth and adorneth the garden, and heighteneth the effect thereof. In like manner, when divers shades of thought, temperament and character, are brought together under the power and influence of one central agency, the beauty and glory of human perfection will be revealed and made manifest. Naught but the ce-*

*lestial potency of the Word of God, which ruleth and transcendeth the realities of all things, is capable of harmonizing the divergent thoughts, sentiments, ideas and convictions of the children of men.*

—'Abdu'l-Bahá

(Quoted in *The World Order of Bahá'u'lláh*, p. 42)

*The diversity in the human family should be the cause of love and harmony, as it is in music where many different notes blend together in the making of a perfect chord.*

—'Abdu'l-Bahá

(*Paris Talks*, no. 15.7)

*Consider the world of created beings, how varied and diverse they are in species, yet with one sole origin. All the differences that appear are those of outward form and color. This diversity of type is apparent throughout the whole of nature. . . .*

*So it is with humanity. It is made up of many races, and its peoples are of different color, white, black, yellow, brown and red—but they all come from the same God, and all are servants to Him.*—'Abdu'l-Bahá

(*Paris Talks*, no. 15.3–5)

*The whole earth is one home, and all peoples, did they but know it, are bathed in the oneness of God's mercy. God created all. He gives sustenance to all. He guides and trains all under the shadow of his bounty. We must follow the example God Himself gives us, and do away with all disputations and quarrels.* —'Abdu'l-Bahá

(*'Abdu'l-Bahá in London*, p. 38)

## ACQUIRING VIRTUES, LOVING, AND KNOWING

In the Bahá'í Faith, marriage is exalted as an expression of God's divine purpose for humanity. The Bahá'í conception of marriage therefore differs radically from the present popular notion that diminishes the importance of marriage for the family, the basic unit of society, and reduces it to a transitory arrangement based on romantic illusion or expediency. The consequences of this misconception have been tragic and far-reaching. Not only do the children from such marriages suffer, but the marriage partners themselves, having failed to discover the spiritual purpose and potential of marriage, often subject themselves to intolerable duress, become apathetic, or go through the trauma of divorce.

In order that we might experience the true fulfillment of marriage and avoid many of the needlessly self-destructive practices of a collapsing social order, Bahá'u'lláh and 'Abdu'l-Bahá have given us prescriptions for acquiring the virtues on which a spiritual marital union depends and have explained how the capacities of knowing and loving God sustain the marriage relationship.

In essence, to know and love God means to learn of His attributes from His Manifestation, Bahá'u'lláh, and to reflect those attributes by submitting to His will and obeying His laws and teachings. By striving to reflect the attributes of God in all of our interactions, including those with our marriage partner, we will be able to create and sustain a spiritual union, and it will enable us to draw nearer to God.

*Give ear unto the verses of God which He Who is the sacred Lote-*

*Tree reciteth unto you. They are assuredly the infallible balance, established by God, the Lord of this world and the next. Through them the soul of man is caused to wing its flight towards the Dayspring of Revelation, and the heart of every true believer is suffused with light. Such are the laws which God hath enjoined upon you, such His commandments prescribed unto you in His Holy Tablet; obey them with joy and gladness, for this is best for you, did ye but know.*

—Bahá'u'lláh

(The Kitáb-i-Aqdas, ¶148)

*From amongst all mankind hath He chosen you, and your eyes have been opened to the light of guidance and your ears attuned to the music of the Company above. . . .*

*To thank Him for this, make ye a mighty effort, and choose for yourselves a noble goal. Through the power of faith, obey ye the teachings of God, and let all your actions conform to His laws.*
—'Abdu'l-Bahá

(*Selections from the Writings of 'Abdu'l-Bahá*, no. 17.2–3)

*The perfections of God, the divine virtues, are reflected or revealed in the human reality. Just as the light and effulgence of the sun when cast upon a polished mirror are reflected fully, gloriously, so, likewise, the qualities and attributes of Divinity are radiated from the depths of a pure human heart.*—'Abdu'l-Bahá

(*The Promulgation of Universal Peace*, p. 95)

*Every man imbued with divine qualities, who reflects heavenly moralities and perfections, who is the expression of ideal and praiseworthy attributes, is, verily, in the image and likeness of God.*—'Abdu'l-Bahá

(*The Promulgation of Universal Peace*, p. 96)

— 2 —

# The Foundation of Spiritual Union

If our true reality is spiritual rather than physical, the most important and enduring of our human relationships will also be spiritual in nature. Creating a marital relationship that will become progressively spiritualized depends upon conscious and sincere efforts to understand the principles underlying the foundations of spiritual union and to translate them into *"reality and action."**

Of course, marriage is a physical relationship as well; but, as 'Abdu'l-Bahá explains, in order for the union to be an enduring one, the physical relationship must be established on the spiritual one.

> *Marriage, among the mass of the people, is a physical bond, and this union can only be temporary, since it is foredoomed to a physical separation at the close.*
>
> *Among the people of Bahá, however, marriage must be a union of the body and of the spirit as well, for here both husband and wife are aglow with the same wine, both are*

---

* Bahá'u'lláh, *Gleanings from the Writings of Bahá'u'lláh,* no. 117.1.

*enamored of the same matchless Face, both live and move through the same spirit, both are illumined by the same glory. This connection between them is a spiritual one, hence it is a bond that will abide forever. Likewise do they enjoy strong and lasting ties in the physical world as well, for if the marriage is based both on the spirit and the body, that union is a true one, hence it will endure. If, however, the bond is physical and nothing more, it is sure to be only temporary, and must inexorably end in separation.*

*When, therefore, the people of Bahá undertake to marry, the union must be a true relationship, a spiritual coming together as well as a physical one, so that throughout every phase of life, and in all the worlds of God, their union will endure; for this real oneness is a gleaming out of the love of God.*—'Abdu'l-Bahá

(*Selections from the Writings of 'Abdu'l-Bahá*, no. 84.2–4)

*Wherefore must the friends of God, with utter sanctity, with one accord, rise up in the spirit, in unity with one another, to such a degree that they will become even as one being and one soul. On such a plane as this, physical bodies play no part, rather doth the spirit take over and rule; and when its power encompasseth all then is spiritual union achieved. Strive ye by day and night to cultivate your unity to the fullest degree.*—'Abdu'l-Bahá

(*Selections from the Writings of 'Abdu'l-Bahá*, no. 174.5)

*The institution of marriage, as established by Bahá'u'lláh, while giving due importance to the physical aspect of marital union considers it as subordinate to the moral and spiritual purposes and functions with which it has been invested by an all-wise and loving Providence.*
—Shoghi Effendi
(*Lights of Guidance*, no. 754)

Fundamentally, such a *"spiritual relationship and everlasting union"* depends upon knowledge of and submission to the will of God. This is the foundation of a spiritual union.

*The source of all good is trust in God, submission unto His command, and contentment with His holy will and pleasure.*

—Bahá'u'lláh

(*Tablets of Bahá'u'lláh*, p. 155)

*O Son of Man! Wert thou to speed through the immensity of space and traverse the expanse of heaven, yet thou wouldst find no rest save in submission to Our command and humbleness before Our Face.*

—Bahá'u'lláh

(The Hidden Words, Arabic, no. 40)

*Say: True liberty consisteth in man's submission unto My commandments, little as ye know it.*

—Bahá'u'lláh

(The Kitáb-i-Aqdas, ¶125)

## SUBMISSION TO THE WILL OF GOD

When a man and woman marry in the Bahá'í Faith, each says to the other, before witnesses:

> *We will all, verily, abide by the Will of God.*—Bahá'u'lláh
>
> (*The Kitáb-i-Aqdas, Questions and Answers*, no. 3)

Although the vow is simple and short, its meaning is profound. It affirms the fact that marriage is not only a contract between two people. It involves their relationship with God; it is a social and spiritual concern of the Bahá'í community; and it offers a model to society at large. Therefore when we enter Bahá'í marriage, we establish a relationship with God consistent with the values we share with the members of our Bahá'í community. The marriage relationship is thus based upon a mutual agreement that the primary point of its unity and the central determinant of its organization and functioning is submission to the will of God as expressed by Bahá'u'lláh in this Day. When two people agree on and submit to the same principles, they have both freedom and unity in their relationship. If one submits his or her will to the other, rather than both submitting to God's will, neither is free, and the union is manmade rather than spiritual. It is out of touch with reality and may be unstable or even destructive.

Thus the marriage vow expresses the immutable foundation of a spiritual union. When two people base their marriage on abiding *"by the Will of God,"* most of the serious difficulties the marriage encounters will come from outside the marriage rather than from within it. Such difficulties are more easily resolved because the strength of each partner is free to be focused on the problem, rather than being dissipated on internal conflicts.

## LOVE OF GOD

For a union to be maintained, a power of attraction must operate to hold two people together. 'Abdu'l-Bahá explains that the basic cohesive force in the universe is love,* and he elaborates on its several forms:

---

* "*Love is the most great law that ruleth this mighty and heavenly cycle, the unique power that bindeth together the divers elements of this material world, the supreme magnetic force that directeth the movements of the spheres in the celestial realms.*"—'Abdu'l-Bahá, *Selections from the Writings of 'Abdu'l-Bahá,* no. 12.1.

*There are four kinds of love. The first is the love that flows from God to man; it consists of the inexhaustible graces, the Divine effulgence and heavenly illumination. Through this love the world of being receives life. Through this love man is endowed with physical existence, until, through the breath of the Holy Spirit—this same love—he receives eternal life and becomes the image of the Living God. This love is the origin of all the love in the world of creation.*

*The second is the love that flows from man to God. This is faith, attraction to the Divine, enkindlement, progress, entrance into the Kingdom of God, receiving the Bounties of God, illumination with the lights of the Kingdom. This love is the origin of all philanthropy; this love causes the hearts of men to reflect the rays of the Sun of Reality.*

*The third is the love of God towards the Self or Identity of God. This is the transfiguration of His Beauty, the reflection of Himself in the mirror of His Creation. This is the reality of love, the Ancient Love, the Eternal Love. Through one ray of this Love all other love exists.*

*The fourth is the love of man for man. The love which exists between the hearts of believers is prompted by the ideal of the unity of spirits. This love is attained through the knowledge of God, so that men see the Divine Love reflected in the heart. Each sees in the other the Beauty of God reflected in the soul, and finding this point of similarity, they are*

*attracted to one another in love. This love will make all men the waves of one sea, this love will make them all the stars of one heaven and the fruits of one tree. This love will bring the realization of true accord, the foundation of real unity.*—'Abdu'l-Bahá
(*Paris Talks*, no. 58.4–7)

Recognizing the love of God to be the true source of love among people, partners in marriage should seek the sustenance of their love for each other in their love of God. Happiness in marriage depends on it.

*The utterance of God is a lamp, whose light is these words: Ye are the fruits of one tree, and the leaves of one branch. Deal ye one with an-*

*other with the utmost love and harmony, with friendliness and fellowship.*—Bahá'u'lláh

(*Gleanings from the Writings of Bahá'u'lláh*, no. 132.3)

*If any differences arise amongst you, behold Me standing before your face, and overlook the faults of one another for My name's sake and as a token of your love for My manifest and resplendent Cause.*—Bahá'u'lláh

(*Gleanings from the Writings of Bahá'u'lláh*, no. 146.1)

*What a power is love! It is the most wonderful, the greatest of all living powers.*

*Love gives life to the lifeless. Love lights a flame in the heart that is*

*cold. Love brings hope to the hopeless and gladdens the hearts of the sorrowful.*

*In the world of existence there is indeed no greater power than the power of love. When the heart of man is aglow with the flame of love, he is ready to sacrifice all—even his life. In the Gospel it is said God is love.*—'Abdu'l-Bahá

(*Paris Talks*, no. 58.1–3)

*You will never become angry or impatient if you love them for the sake of God. . . . There are imperfections in every human being, and you will always become unhappy if you look toward the people themselves. But if you look toward God, you will love them and be kind to them, for the*

*world of God is the world of perfection and complete mercy.*
—'Abdu'l-Bahá

(*The Promulgation of Universal Peace*, p. 128)

*When you love a member of your family or a compatriot, let it be with a ray of the Infinite Love! Let it be in God, and for God! Wherever you find the attributes of God love that person, whether he be of your family or of another. Shed the light of a boundless love on every human being whom you meet, whether of your country, your race, your political party, or of any other nation, color or shade of political opinion. Heaven will support you while you work in this ingathering of the scat-*

*tered peoples of the world beneath the shadow of the almighty tent of unity.*—'Abdu'l-Bahá

(*Paris Talks*, no. 9.21)

## LOYALTY, CHASTITY, AND DETACHMENT

The fundamental qualities that link the soul with God—loyalty and faithfulness—must also become the foundation binding lovers together in marriage. The most precious expression of this loyalty and faithfulness to God and to each other is chastity before marriage and faithfulness after marriage.*

* *"Chastity—one of the rarest of all moral gems in the world to-day—means to conserve your personal sex powers, so intimate in nature, capable of conferring so much beauty on your life, for their proper expression which is with your life partner. . . ."* —Rúḥíyyih Rabbani, *Prescription for Living*, p. 70.

*Purity and chastity have been, and still are, the most great ornaments for the handmaidens of God. God is My Witness! The brightness of the light of chastity sheddeth its illumination upon the worlds of the spirit, and its fragrance is wafted even unto the Most Exalted Paradise.*
—Bahá'u'lláh

(Quoted in *The Advent of Divine Justice*, ¶48)

*A chaste and holy life must be made the controlling principle in the behavior and conduct of all Bahá'ís, both in their social relations with the members of their own community, and in their contact with the world at large. It must adorn and reinforce the ceaseless labors and meritorious exertions of those whose enviable*

*position is to propagate the Message, and to administer the affairs, of the Faith of Bahá'u'lláh.*
—Shoghi Effendi
(*The Advent of Divine Justice*, ¶46)

*Chastity implies both before and after marriage an unsullied, chaste sex life. Before marriage absolutely chaste, after marriage absolutely faithful to one's chosen companion. Faithful in all sexual acts, faithful in word and in deed.*
—On behalf of Shoghi Effendi
(*Lights of Guidance*, no. 1212)

*The Bahá'í Teachings on this matter* [sex and its relation to marriage] . . . *are very clear and emphatic. Briefly stated the Bahá'í conception of sex is based on the belief that chastity should be strictly practiced by both sexes, not only because it is in itself highly commendable ethically, but also due to its being the only way to a happy and successful marital life. Sex relationships of any form, outside marriage, are not permissible therefore, and whoso violates this rule will not only be responsible to God, but will incur the necessary punishment from society.*

*The Bahá'í Faith recognizes the value of the sex impulse, but condemns its illegitimate and improper expression such as free love, companionate marriage and others, all of which it considers positively harmful to man and to the society in which he lives. The proper use of the sex instinct is the natural right of every individual, and it is precisely for this very purpose that the institution of marriage has been established. The Bahá'ís do not believe in the suppression of the sex impulse but in its regulation and control.*

—On behalf of Shoghi Effendi
(*The Compilation of Compilations,* 1.145)

*As to chastity, this is one of the most challenging concepts to get across in this very permissive age, but Bahá'ís must make the utmost effort to uphold Bahá'í standards, no matter how difficult they may seem at first. Such efforts will be made easier if the youth will understand that the laws and standards of the Faith are meant to free them from untold spiritual and moral difficulties in the same way that a proper appreciation of the laws of*

> *nature enables one to live in harmony with the forces of the planet.*
>
> —On behalf of the Universal House of Justice
>
> (*Lights of Guidance*, no. 1216)

Far from advocating asceticism, the Bahá'í teachings seek to preserve the inherent beauty and richness in the sexual relationship of husband and wife. Chastity protects this beauty, while promiscuity diminishes sex as a spontaneous and genuine expression of communion and love.

> *It must be remembered, however, that the maintenance of such a high standard of moral conduct is not to be associated or confused with any form of asceticism, or of excessive and bigoted puritanism. The stan-*

> *dard inculcated by Bahá'u'lláh seeks, under no circumstances, to deny anyone the legitimate right and privilege to derive the fullest advantage and benefit from the manifold joys, beauties, and pleasures with which the world has been so plentifully enriched by an All-Loving Creator.*
> —Shoghi Effendi
> (*The Advent of Divine Justice,* ¶50)

What 'Abdu'l-Bahá and Shoghi Effendi mean by chastity is not merely the absence of certain behaviors. Chastity also entails an attitude toward personal relationships that involves a responsibility to foster others' spiritual development as well as one's own.*

* *"The true marriage of Bahá'ís is this, that husband and wife should be united both physically and spiritually, that they may ever improve*

Chastity also implies moderation:

*Such a chaste and holy life, with its implications of modesty, purity, temperance, decency, and clean-mindedness, involves no less than the exercise of moderation in all that pertains to dress, language, amusements, and all artistic and literary avocations. It demands daily vigilance in the control of one's carnal desires and corrupt inclinations. It calls for the abandonment of a frivolous conduct, with its excessive attachment to trivial and often misdirected pleasures. It requires total*

---

*the spiritual life of each other, and may enjoy everlasting unity throughout all the worlds of God. This is Bahá'í marriage."* —'Abdu'l-Bahá, *Selections from the Writings of 'Abdu'l-Bahá*, no. 86.2.

*abstinence from all alcoholic drinks, from opium, and from similar habit-forming drugs. It condemns the prostitution of art and of literature, the practices of nudism and of companionate marriage, infidelity in marital relationships, and all manner of promiscuity, of easy familiarity, and of sexual vices. It can tolerate no compromise with the theories, the standards, the habits, and the excesses of a decadent age. Nay rather it seeks to demonstrate, through the dynamic force of its example, the pernicious character of such theories, the falsity of such standards, the hollowness of such claims, the perversity of such habits, and the sacrilegious character of such excesses.*

—Shoghi Effendi

(*The Advent of Divine Justice,* ¶47)

Chastity is also the emblem of detachment.

> *And if he* [My true follower] *met the fairest and most comely of women, he would not feel his heart seduced by the least shadow of desire for her beauty. Such an one indeed is the creation of spotless chastity. Thus instructeth you the Pen of the Ancient of Days, as bidden by your Lord, the Almighty, the All-Bountiful.*
>
> —Bahá'u'lláh
>
> (Quoted in *The Advent of Divine Justice,* ¶48)

Detachment and love of God lead to true happiness. They free marriage partners to serve mankind and to help raise up a new race of people. In so doing they create a spiritual unity markedly absent in a relationship with lesser goals.

> *It behooveth the people of Bahá to die to the world and all that is therein, to be so detached from all earthly things that the inmates of Paradise may inhale from their garment the sweet smelling savor of sanctity.*
> —Bahá'u'lláh
>
> (Quoted in *The Advent of Divine Justice,* ¶48)

> *O ye the beloved of the one true God! Pass beyond the narrow retreats of your evil and corrupt desires, and advance into the vast immensity of the realm of God, and abide ye in the meads of sanctity and of detachment, that the fragrance of your deeds may lead the whole of man-*

*kind to the ocean of God's unfading glory.*—Bahá'u'lláh

(Quoted in *The Advent of Divine Justice,* ¶48)

*A race of men, incomparable in character, shall be raised up which, with the feet of detachment, will tread under all who are in heaven and on earth, and will cast the sleeve of holiness over all that hath been created from water and clay.*
—Bahá'u'lláh

(Quoted in *The Advent of Divine Justice,* ¶48)

*Our greatest efforts must be directed towards detachment from the things of the world; we must strive to become more spiritual, more luminous, to follow the counsel of the Divine Teaching, to serve the cause of unity and true equality, to be merciful, to reflect the love of the Highest on all men, so that the light of the Spirit shall be apparent in all our deeds, to the end that all humanity shall be united, the stormy sea thereof calmed, and all rough waves disappear from off the surface of life's ocean henceforth unruffled and peaceful.*—'Abdu'l-Bahá

(*Paris Talks*, no. 28.19)

## EQUALITY OF MEN AND WOMEN

A spiritual marriage depends upon the equal participation and sharing of responsibilities of both the man and the woman. There can be no double standards; spiritual principles apply to both men and women. 'Abdu'l-Bahá made several statements to clarify the Bahá'í principle of the equality of men and women:

> *Women and men have been and will always be equal in the sight of God. . . . Verily God created women for men, and men for women.*
> —Bahá'u'lláh
> (*The Compilation of Compilations*, 2:2145)

> *The happiness of mankind will be realized when women and men coordinate and advance equally, for each is the complement and helpmeet of the other.*—'Abdu'l-Bahá
> (*Promulgation of Universal Peace*, p. 253)

> *Woman must endeavor then to attain greater perfection, to be man's equal in every respect, to make progress in all in which she has been backward,*

*so that man will be compelled to acknowledge her equality of capacity and attainment.*—'Abdu'l-Bahá

(*Paris Talks*, no. 50.11)

*The world of humanity is possessed of two wings: the male and the female. So long as these two wings are not equivalent in strength, the bird will not fly. Until womankind reaches the same degree as man, until she enjoys the same arena of activity, extraordinary attainment for humanity will not be realized; humanity cannot wing its way to heights of real attainment. When the two wings or parts become equivalent in strength, enjoying the same prerogatives, the flight of man will be exceedingly lofty and extraordinary. Therefore, woman must receive the same education as man and all inequality be adjusted. Thus, imbued with the same virtues as man, rising through all the degrees of human attainment, women will become the peers of men, and until this equality is established, true progress and attainment for the human race will not be facilitated.*—'Abdu'l-Bahá

(*The Promulgation of Universal Peace*, pp. 529–30)

*Divine Justice demands that the rights of both sexes should be equally respected since neither is superior to the other. . . . Dignity before God depends, not on sex, but on purity and luminosity of heart. Human virtues belong equally to all!*
—'Abdu'l-Bahá

(*Paris Talks*, no. 50.10)

Equality does not mean that functions or roles must be identical; rather it implies that both men and women must contribute equally in marriage and in society.

> *According to the spirit of this age, women must advance and fulfill their mission in all departments of life, becoming equal to men. They must be on the same level as men and enjoy equal rights. This is my earnest prayer and it is one of the fundamental principles of Bahá'u'lláh.*
> —'Abdu'l-Bahá
>
> (Quoted in *Bahá'u'lláh and the New Era*, p. 162)

> *The education of women is of greater importance than the education of men, for they are the mothers of the race, and mothers rear the chil-*

*dren. The first teachers of children are the mothers. Therefore, they must be capably trained in order to educate both sons and daughters. There are many provisions in the words of Bahá'u'lláh in regard to this.*

*He promulgated the adoption of the same course of education for man and woman. Daughters and sons must follow the same curriculum of study, thereby promoting unity of the sexes.*—'Abdu'l-Bahá
(*The Promulgation of Universal Peace,* p. 243)

*This principle* [of the equality of the sexes] *is far more than the enunciation of admirable ideals; it has profound implications in all aspects of human relations and must be an integral element of Bahá'í domestic and community life. The application of this principle gives rise to changes in habits and practices which have prevailed for many centuries.*

—The Universal House of Justice

(An unpublished letter January 24, 1993, to an individual)

The Bahá'í wedding vow, the statement said by both the man and the woman, commits the bride and groom to each other, and to working toward equality and unity by submitting themselves to God's will. A Bahá'í marriage is based upon mutual respect, spiritual harmony, and reliance on God. By understanding and focusing on the spiritual attributes of marriage, a couple is able to build a strong foundation and a lasting union.

— 3 —

# The Purpose of Marriage

Beyond creating a "fortress for well-being" and improving the spiritual life of one another, another important aspect of marriage is the procreation and education of children. By focusing on children's spiritual education from the very beginning of their lives, they will be raised to know God and to observe the laws revealed by Bahá'u'lláh.

*Enter ye into wedlock, that after you another may arise in your stead.*
—Bahá'u'lláh

(*Epistle to the Son of the Wolf*, p. 49)

*But for man, who, on My earth, would remember Me, and how could My attributes and My names be revealed?*—Bahá'u'lláh

(*Epistle to the Son of the Wolf*, p. 49)

*O peerless Lord! In Thine almighty wisdom Thou hast enjoined marriage upon the peoples, that the generations of men may succeed one another in this contingent world, and that ever, so long as the world shall last, they may busy themselves at the Threshold of Thy oneness with servi-*

*tude and worship, with salutation, adoration and praise.*

—'Abdu'l-Bahá

(*Bahá'í Prayers*, pp. 118–19)

*Train these children with divine exhortations. From their childhood instill in their hearts the love of God so they may manifest in their lives the fear of God and have confidence in the bestowals of God. Teach them to free themselves from human imperfections and to acquire the divine perfections latent in the heart of man. The life of man is useful if he attains the perfections of man. If he becomes the center of the imperfections of the world of humanity, death is better than life, and nonexistence better than existence.*

*Therefore, make ye an effort in order that these children may be rightly trained and educated and that each one of them may attain perfection in the world of humanity. Know ye the value of these children, for they are all my children.*—'Abdu'l-Bahá

(*The Promulgation of Universal Peace*, p. 73)

*The Bahá'í Teachings do not only encourage marital life, considering it the natural and normal way of existence for every sane, healthy and socially-conscious and responsible person, but raise marriage to the status of a divine institution, its chief and sacred purpose being the perpetuation of the human race—which is the very flower of the entire cre-*

*ation—and its elevation to the true station destined for it by God.*
—On behalf of Shoghi Effendi
(*The Compilation of Compilations*, 2:2316)

Parenthood is the first and foremost duty for a husband and wife, and it is this aspect of marriage that is perhaps most closely linked with fulfilling God's purpose for humanity. Since the most effective way of imparting to children an understanding of God's purpose for humanity is through example, the goal is clear to Bahá'í parents.

Apprehending God's purpose for humanity should be at the heart of parenthood. Two aspects of apprehending this purpose that are essential to the role of a parent are knowing and loving God (through recognizing, obeying, knowing, and loving His Manifestation and His creation) and acquiring virtues (through purification of one's character and motives). Parents can promote the oneness of mankind by teaching children to love God and by helping them to develop an attitude of worldmindedness free from racial, ethnic, or religious prejudices. By providing their children with divine education and examples of spiritual men and women to emulate, parents help to carry forward an ever-advancing civilization, which depends on the raising up of succeeding generations who have acquired those virtues on which a spiritualized society depends.

> *The education and training of children is among the most meritorious acts of humankind and draweth*

*down the grace and favor of the All-Merciful, for education is the indispensable foundation of all human excellence and alloweth man to work his way to the heights of abiding glory. If a child be trained from his infancy, he will, through the loving care of the Holy Gardener, drink in the crystal waters of the spirit and of knowledge, like a young tree amid the rilling brooks. And certainly he will gather to himself the bright rays of the Sun of Truth, and through its light and heat will grow ever fresh and fair in the garden of life.*
—'Abdu'l-Bahá

(*Selections from the Writings of 'Abdu'l-Bahá*, no. 103.1)

*While the children are yet in their infancy feed them from the breast of heavenly grace, foster them in the cradle of all excellence, rear them in the embrace of bounty. Give them the advantage of every useful kind of knowledge. Let them share in every new and rare and wondrous craft and art. Bring them up to work and strive, and accustom them to hardship. Teach them to dedicate their lives to matters of great import, and inspire them to undertake studies that will benefit mankind.*

—'Abdu'l-Bahá

(*Selections from the Writings of 'Abdu'l-Bahá*, no. 102.3)

*Know ye that in God's sight, the best of all ways to worship Him is to educate the children and train them in all the perfections of humankind;*

*and no nobler deed than this can be imagined.*—'Abdu'l-Bahá

(*Selections from the Writings of 'Abdu'l-Bahá*, no. 114.1)

*Regarding the education of children: it behooveth thee to nurture them at the breast of the love of God, and urge them onward to the things of the spirit, that they may turn their faces unto God; that their ways may conform to the rules of good conduct and their character be second to none; that they make their own all the graces and praiseworthy qualities of humankind; acquire a sound knowledge of the various branches of learning, so that from the very beginning of life they may become spiritual beings, dwellers in the Kingdom, enamored of the sweet breaths of holiness, and may receive an education religious, spiritual, and of the Heavenly Realm.*—'Abdu'l-Bahá

(*Selections from the Writings of 'Abdu'l-Bahá*, no. 122.1)

*To train the character of humankind is one of the weightiest commandments of God, and the influence of such training is the same as that which the sun exerteth over tree and fruit. Children must be most carefully watched over, protected and trained; in such consisteth true parenthood and parental mercy.*
—'Abdu'l-Bahá

(*The Compilation of Compilations*, 1:590)

*No matter how far the world of humanity advances, it fails to attain*

*the highest degree unless quickened by the education and divine bestowals of the Holy Spirit. This ensures human progress and prosperity.*
—'Abdu'l-Bahá

(*The Promulgation of Universal Peace*, p. 288)

# Part II

# PREPARATIONS FOR MARRIAGE IN LIGHT OF GOD'S PURPOSE FOR HUMANITY

— 4 —

# Bahá'í Engagement

It is a heavenly bounty to be able to understand the nature and purpose of marriage, for one can then make adequate preparation for it. The importance of preparation for marriage and its challenges cannot be overstressed. By preparing for marriage and entering into wedlock with a unified vision, couples will be able to work together to overcome challenges that arise during marriage.

## KNOWING EACH OTHER—KNOWING ONESELF

Before entering into marriage, it is important for one to know oneself. Knowing oneself allows one to drawn nearer to God. If one does not know oneself, one will constantly be making decisions that may harm one's life or making commitments that one has trouble honoring. Furthermore, not knowing oneself will make it difficult to accurately judge the character of another. Thus one who does not know oneself is not well prepared for engagement and marriage.

*He hath known God who hath known himself.*—Bahá'u'lláh

(*Gleanings from the Writings of Bahá'u'lláh*, no. 90.1)

*Man should know his own self and recognize that which leadeth unto*

*loftiness or lowliness, glory or abasement, wealth or poverty.*
—Bahá'u'lláh

(*Tablets of Bahá'u'lláh*, p. 35)

*God has given man the eye of investigation by which he may see and recognize truth. . . . Man is not intended to see through the eyes of another, hear through another's ears nor comprehend with another's brain. Each human creature has individual endowment, power and responsibility in the creative plan of God. Therefore, depend upon your own reason and judgment and adhere to the outcome of your own investigation. . . .*
—'Abdu'l-Bahá

(*Promulgation of Universal Peace*, p. 409)

Beyond knowing oneself, of critical importance in preparation for marriage is becoming informed of the character of one's intended spouse:

> *Bahá'í marriage is the commitment of the two parties one to the other, and their mutual attachment of mind and heart. Each must, however, exercise the utmost care to become thoroughly acquainted with the character of the other, that the binding covenant between them may be a tie that will endure forever. Their purpose must be this: to become loving companions and comrades and at one with each other for time and eternity. . . .* — 'Abdu'l-Bahá
>
> (*Selections from the Writings of 'Abdu'l-Bahá*, no. 86.1)

*Bahá'í law places the responsibility for ascertaining knowledge of the*

*character of those entering into the marriage contract on the two parties involved, and on the parents, who must give consent to the marriage.*
—The Universal House of Justice
(*Lights of Guidance*, no. 1231)

*A couple should study each other's character and spend time getting to know each other before they decide to marry, and when they do marry it should be with the intention of establishing an eternal bond.*
—On behalf of the Universal House of Justice
(*Lights of Guidance*, no. 1269)

Unfortunately today's dating practices may make it easy to avoid getting to know another person. The conditions under which dating couples associate, involving diversions, game playing, and entertainment, are not necessarily the best ones for assessing character. Indeed for many people the function of dating is to conceal one's real self. It is hardly surprising that persons who marry after such a courtship become disillusioned when they begin to live together in the real world of home building and child-rearing.

> *The love which sometimes exists between friends is not (true) love, because it is subject to transmutation; this is merely fascination. . . .*
>
> *Today you will see two souls apparently in close friendship; tomorrow all this may be changed. Yesterday they were ready to die for one another, today they shun one another's society! This is not love; it*

*is the yielding of the hearts to the accidents of life. When that which has caused this "love" to exist passes, the love passes also. . . .*— 'Abdu'l-Bahá
(*Paris Talks*, no. 58.8–9)

*One of the signs of a decadent society, a sign which is very evident in the world today, is an almost frenetic devotion to pleasure and diversion, an insatiable thirst for amusement, a fanatical devotion to games and sport, a reluctance to treat any matter seriously, and a scornful, derisory attitude towards virtue and solid worth. Abandonment of "a frivolous conduct" does not imply that a Bahá'í must be sour-faced or perpetually solemn. Humour, happiness, joy are characteristics of a true Bahá'í life. Frivolity palls and*

> *eventually leads to boredom and emptiness, but true happiness and joy and humour that are parts of a balanced life that includes serious thought, compassion and humble servitude to God, are characteristics that enrich life and add to its radiance.*
>
> —On behalf of the Universal House of Justice
>
> (*The Compilation of Compilations*, 1:138)

Since the goal of the union of a man and woman is to serve God together, the best way to become informed of the character of the person with whom one is contemplating marriage is to engage in some form of work and service together. This will provide many opportunities to assess one's own maturity and readiness for marriage, and one will come to know the character and values of one's prospective marriage partner. If both share similar values and are deepened spiritually, the chances are that they will be able to build a successful marriage. A decision to become engaged before becoming informed of each other's character is premature and unwise. Hardly any decision in life is more critical than the decision to marry someone, and no decision is more dependent for its success on self-knowledge and upon the ability to judge the character of someone else than is this one. One way to assess a potential spouse's character is by observing his or her reliance on the writings of the Faith to guide his or her life.

> *The foundation of all their* [Bahá'ís] *other accomplishments is their study of the teachings, the spiritualiza-*

*tion of their lives and the forming of their characters in accordance with the standards of Bahá'u'lláh. As the moral standards of the people around us collapse and decay . . . the Bahá'ís must increasingly stand out as pillars of righteousness and forbearance. The life of a Bahá'í will be characterized by truthfulness and decency; he will walk uprightly among his fellowmen, dependent upon none save God, yet linked by bonds of love and brotherhood with all mankind; he will be entirely detached from the loose standards, the decadent theories, the frenetic experimentation, the desperation of present-day society, will look upon his neighbors with a bright and friendly face and be a beacon light and a haven for all*

*those who would emulate his strength of character and assurance of soul.*
—The Universal House of Justice
(*Messages from the Universal House of Justice, 1963–1986*, no. 37.5)

At times the attraction between two souls can take the form of an unhealthy emotional dependence, making it very difficult to become informed of one another's true character. Such an attachment blinds the eye and enables one to sustain the relationship while ignoring those many indicators in his own behavior and in that of the other person that are symptomatic of immaturity or irresponsibility.* If, for instance, one finds

* Parents are frequently able to sense such attachments and their power to impair the abil-

him or herself rationalizing, justifying, or ignoring behavior that is contrary to Bahá'í law, this is a sign that the obscuring forces of attachment are at work. That there may be a powerful attraction between two souls contemplating marriage is not questioned; but if that attraction is based on romantic illusion or neurotic attachment, it will usually decrease one's capacity to assess readiness for marriage in light of the Bahá'í teachings. It also frequently involves giving up part of one's identity or permitting oneself to be manipulated into behavior inconsistent with one's spiritual reality and not in keeping with God's purpose

---

ity to make a sound decision concerning engagement and marriage. The obligation to obtain parental consent to marriage may, in such instances, protect one from an unwise choice.

for humanity. If an attachment to another can so weaken a person that he or she will indulge in behavior not in keeping with that purpose, this is a sure sign that there is a lack of spiritual maturity and readiness for marriage.

> *Disencumber yourselves of all attachment to this world and the vanities thereof. Beware that ye approach them not, inasmuch as they prompt you to walk after your own lusts and covetous desires, and hinder you from entering the straight and glorious Path.*—Bahá'u'lláh
>
> (*Gleanings from the Writings of Bahá'u'lláh*, no. 128.3)

> *Walk not with the ungodly and seek not fellowship with him, for such*

*companionship turneth the radiance of the heart into infernal fire.*
—Bahá'u'lláh
(The Hidden Words, Persian, no. 57)

## DETACHMENT

It is, in truth, detachment that will enable one to become informed of another's character. Being detached is in itself a sign of spiritual maturity. In its spiritual meaning, detachment does not refer to being cool, aloof, or distant. It means being relatively free from having one's feelings or thoughts controlled or determined by someone else. It is quite possible for one to be strongly and warmly attracted to another human being, while at the same time one is detached in a spiritual sense. Such detachment preserves one's identity; it also protects one from gullibility and blindness in assessing one's own motives as well as the motives of others. It brings strength, independence, stability, and self-knowledge. Detachment comes from turning toward God and cultivating an awareness of His purpose for humanity.

> *Detachment is as the sun; in whatsoever heart it doth shine it quencheth the fire of covetousness and self. He whose sight is illumined with the light of understanding will assuredly detach himself from the world and the vanities thereof.* —Bahá'u'lláh
>
> (Published in *The Divine Art of Living*, p. 67)

*Adorn the heads of Thy loved ones with the crown of detachment and*

*attire their temples with the raiment of righteousness.*
—Bahá'u'lláh
(*Tablets of Bahá'u'lláh*, p. 57)

*Piety and detachment are even as two most great luminaries of the heaven of teaching. Blessed the one who hath attained unto this supreme station, this habitation of transcendent holiness and sublimity.*
—Bahá'u'lláh
(*Tablets of Bahá'u'lláh*, p. 253)

*Well is it with him who hath been illumined with the light of trust and detachment.*—Bahá'u'lláh
(*Epistle to the Son of the Wolf*, p. 147)

*Blessed are they that have soared on the wings of detachment and attained the station which, as ordained by God, overshadoweth the entire creation, whom neither the vain imaginations of the learned, nor the multitude of the hosts of the earth have succeeded in deflecting from His Cause. Who is there among you, O people, who will renounce the world, and draw nigh unto God, the Lord of all names?*—Bahá'u'lláh

(*Gleanings from the Writings of Bahá'u'lláh*, no. 14.18)

## HONESTY AND TRUSTWORTHINESS

Detachment, then, is perhaps the most important prerequisite for making objective judgments while becoming informed of another's character. It enables one, under a variety of different circumstances, to be sensitive to all of the implications for married life of one's own reactions and of the reactions of the other person. For instance, working together with someone else will provide many opportunities for determining whether that person is fundamentally honest and trustworthy. Without these traits there can be no integrity, and without integrity there is no basis for a stable and happy relationship. Evidence of lying or dishonesty is a sound reason for questioning an individual's maturity and readiness for marriage. Ignoring such evidence inevitably leads to heart-break and pain.

> *Beautify your tongues, O people, with truthfulness, and adorn your souls with the ornament of honesty.*
> —Bahá'u'lláh
>
> (*Gleanings from the Writings of Bahá'u'lláh*, no. 136.6)

*The light of a good character surpasseth the light of the sun and the radiance thereof. Whoso attaineth unto it is accounted as a jewel among men. The glory and the upliftment of the world must needs depend upon it.*—Bahá'u'lláh

(*Tablets of Bahá'u'lláh*, p. 36)

*Truthfulness is the foundation of all human virtues. Without truthfulness progress and success, in all of the worlds of God, are impossible for any soul. When this holy attribute is established in man, all the divine qualities will also be acquired.*
—'Abdu'l-Bahá

(Quoted in *The Advent of Divine Justice*, ¶40)

*Should any one of you enter a city, he should become a center of attrac-*

*tion by reason of his sincerity, his faithfulness and love, his honesty and fidelity, his truthfulness and loving-kindness towards all the peoples of the world. . . .*—'Abdu'l-Bahá

(*Selections from the Writings of 'Abdu'l-Bahá*, no. 35.5)

No sound marriage relationship can endure irresponsibility on the part of either partner. Therefore, when one is becoming informed of another's character, sensitivity to the trait of irresponsibility is crucial. If, prior to marriage, a person is irresponsible and unreliable, it is very likely that he or she will carry these habits into the marital relationship. While such a person may change, these habits indicate that he or she is probably not ready for marriage. Reliability and trustworthiness are indispensable to an enduring marital relationship.

*Cling ye to the hem of virtue, and hold fast to the cord of trustworthiness and piety. Concern yourselves with the things that benefit mankind, and not with your corrupt and selfish desires.*—Bahá'u'lláh

(*Epistle to the Son of the Wolf*, p. 29)

*We . . . should on no account slacken our efforts to be loyal, sincere and men of good will. We should at all times manifest our truthfulness and sincerity, nay rather, we must be constant in our faithfulness and trustworthiness, and occupy ourselves in offering prayers for the good of all.*—'Abdu'l-Bahá

(*Selections from the Writings of 'Abdu'l-Bahá*, no. 225.30)

*Other attributes of perfection are to fear God, to love God by loving His*

*servants, to exercise mildness and forbearance and calm, to be sincere, amenable, clement and compassionate; to have resolution and courage, trustworthiness and energy, to strive and struggle, to be generous, loyal, without malice, to have zeal and a sense of honor, to be high-minded and magnanimous, and to have regard for the rights of others. Whoever is lacking in these excellent human qualities is defective.*

—'Abdu'l-Bahá

(*The Secret of Divine Civilization*, p. 40)

Since a family usually functions as an economic unit, a responsible attitude toward money, for instance, is important to the stability of marriage. How a person spends his money and what he spends it on indicate his priorities and values, reflecting, for example, a basic generosity or selfishness, wastefulness or wisdom in the use of resources, and a tendency to live only in the present, only in the future, or with a balanced view of both. Wastefulness, selfishness, and a spendthrift enjoyment of the present with no view of future financial obligations or requirements are all symptoms of immaturity in managing finances and certain predictors of marital tensions and difficulties. Miserliness and preoccupation with financial security are equally irresponsible characteristics and may poison the quality of family life.

Preparing for the future while living fully in the present is an important aspect of being a responsible person. One measure of this responsibility is one's attitude toward work. Someone who does not enjoy working and who has no sense of what he would like to do for his life's work will have difficulty in providing for the future. A man or woman who will not or cannot hold a job because of irresponsibility or immaturity cannot in all honesty be considered prepared to assume the responsibilities of marriage.

> *True reliance is for the servant to pursue his profession and calling in this world, to hold fast unto the Lord, to seek naught but His grace, inasmuch as in His Hands is the destiny of all His servants.*—Bahá'u'lláh
>
> (*Tablets of Bahá'u'lláh,* p. 155)

> *O MY SERVANT!*
> *The best of men are they that earn a livelihood by their calling and spend*

*upon themselves and upon their kindred for the love of God, the Lord of all worlds.*—Bahá'u'lláh
(The Hidden Words, Persian, no. 82)

*Thou must endeavor greatly so that thou mayest become unique in thy profession and famous in those parts, because attaining perfection in one's profession in this merciful period is considered to be worship of God. And whilst thou art occupied with thy profession, thou canst remember the True One.*—'Abdu'l-Bahá
(*Selections from the Writings of 'Abdu'l-Bahá*, no. 128.1)

*It is incumbent upon all mankind to become fitted for some useful trade, craft or profession by which subsistence may be assured, and this effi-*

> *ciency is to be considered as an act of worship.*—'Abdu'l-Bahá
> (*The Promulgation of Universal Peace*, p. 612)

## MEETING TESTS

Maturity may also be assessed by observing how a person meets tests or disappointments. If difficulties are usually met by trying to lay the blame elsewhere or by avoiding discussion or analysis of problems, these are danger signals that should not be ignored. Building a marriage and creating a home entail many tests and difficulties. To handle them with equanimity, open-mindedness, forbearance, and patience is essential to the unity of the home and family.

> *But for the tribulations which are sustained in Thy path, how could Thy true lovers be recognized; and were it not for the trials which are*

*borne for love of Thee, how could the station of such as yearn for Thee be revealed? Thy might beareth me witness! The companions of all who adore Thee are the tears they shed, and the comforters of such as seek Thee are the groans they utter, and the food of them who haste to meet Thee is the fragments of their broken hearts.*—Bahá'u'lláh

(*Bahá'í Prayers*, pp. 220–21)

*Bahá'ís should be profoundly aware of the sanctity of marriage and should strive to make their marriages an eternal bond of unity and harmony. This requires effort and sacrifice and wisdom and self-abnegation.*
—On behalf of the Universal House of Justice

(*Lights of Guidance*, no. 1303)

The surest sign of maturity in handling tests and difficulties is a person's willingness to turn to God, to pray, to meditate, and then to make sincere efforts to overcome his or her problems. Being able to handle difficulties in this way is a convincing sign of readiness for marriage.

> *Through the faculty of meditation man attains to eternal life; through it he receives the breath of the Holy Spirit—the bestowal of the Spirit is given in reflection and meditation.*—'Abdu'l-Bahá
>
> (*Paris Talks*, no. 54.11)

> *The prayerful condition is the best of all conditions, for man in such a state communeth with God, especially when prayer is offered in private and*

*at times when one's mind is free, such as at midnight. Indeed, prayer imparteth life.*—'Abdu'l-Bahá

(*Lights of Guidance*, no. 1479)

*There are no set forms of meditation prescribed in the teachings, no plan, as such, for inner development. The friends are urged—nay enjoined—to pray, and they also should meditate, but the manner of doing the latter is left entirely to the individual. . . .*

*The inspiration received through meditation is of a nature that one cannot measure or determine. God can inspire into our minds things that we had no previous knowledge of, if He desires to do so.*

—On behalf of Shoghi Effendi

(*Lights of Guidance*, no. 1482)

*Prayer and meditation are very important factors in deepening the spiritual life of the individual, but with them must go also action and example, as these are the tangible result of the former. Both are essential.*
—On behalf of Shoghi Effendi
(*Lights of Guidance*, no. 1483)

## ASSESSING RELATIONSHIPS WITH OTHERS

Since a strong attachment often blinds one to some aspects of another's character, it is important to observe a prospective mate in her associations with other people and discover what kinds of close friends she has. If a person is unable to treat others with courtesy and respect, chances are that she will not be able to show respect and courtesy within their future home and family. And if the friends she keeps seem to be quite different from her, this is probably a sign that one does not really know her and has not become informed of her true character.

Evidences of possessiveness, covetousness, jealousy, or domineering attitudes are all indicators of immaturity and a lack of readiness for marriage.

*O QUINTESSENCE OF PASSION!*
*Put away all covetousness and seek contentment; for the covetous hath ever been deprived, and the contented hath ever been loved and praised.*
—Bahá'u'lláh
(The Hidden Words, Persian, no. 50)

*We pray God to protect thee from the heat of jealousy and the cold of hatred.*—Bahá'u'lláh
(*Epistle to the Son of the Wolf,* p. 94)

*Verily the most necessary thing is contentment under all circumstances; by this one is preserved from morbid conditions and from lassitude. Yield not to grief and sorrow: they cause the greatest misery. Jealousy consumeth the body and anger doth burn the liver: avoid these two as you would a lion.*—Bahá'u'lláh
(*The Compilation of Compilations,* 1:1020)

*Today all people are immersed in the world of nature. That is why thou dost see jealousy, greed, the struggle for survival, deception, hypocrisy, tyranny, oppression, disputes, strife, bloodshed, looting and pillaging, which all emanate from the world of nature. Few are those who have been freed from this darkness, who have ascended from the world of nature to the world of man, who have followed the divine Teachings, have served the world of humanity, are resplendent, merciful, illumined and like unto a rose garden. Strive thine utmost to become godlike, characterized with His attributes, illumined and merciful, that thou mayest be freed from every bond and become attached at heart to the Kingdom of the incomparable Lord.*

—'Abdu'l-Bahá

(*Selections from the Writings of 'Abdu'l-Bahá*, no. 180.1)

Relationships tend to be stable if people are basically appreciative, sensitive, and fundamentally happy. Furthermore it is a good sign when people have a sense of humor and know how to have fun and laugh together and with others. Such characteristics are signs of maturity and readiness for marriage. Conversely, taking things for granted, seldom laughing, frequently complaining, and failing to show gratitude definitely indicate a lack of readiness. True happiness comes from the realm of the spirit, so if one is dedicated to developing spiritually, one will be truly happy.

> *Happy is the man that pondereth in his heart that which hath been revealed in the Books of God, the Help in Peril, the Self-Subsisting.*
> —Bahá'u'lláh

(*Gleanings from the Writings of Bahá'u'lláh*, no. 10.1)

*As to spiritual happiness, this is the true basis of the life of man, for life is created for happiness, not for sorrow; for pleasure, not for grief. Happiness is life; sorrow is death. Spiritual happiness is life eternal. This is a light which is not followed by darkness. This is an honor which is not followed by shame. This is a life which is not followed by death. This is an existence that is not followed by annihilation. This great blessing and precious gift is obtained by man only through the guidance of God.*—'Abdu'l-Bahá

(Published in *The Divine Art of Living*, p. 18)

*Man is, in reality, a spiritual being, and only when he lives in the spirit is he truly happy.*—'Abdu'l-Bahá

(*Paris Talks*, no. 23.7)

*True happiness depends on spiritual good and having the heart ever open to receive the Divine Bounty.*

*If the heart turns away from the blessings God offers how can it hope for happiness? If it does not put its hope and trust in God's Mercy, where can it find rest? Oh, trust in God! for His Bounty is everlasting, and in His Blessings, for they are superb. Oh! put your faith in the Almighty, for He faileth not and His goodness endureth forever!*—'Abdu'l-Bahá

(*Paris Talks*, no. 34.7–8)

*Happy is the soul that seeketh, in this brilliant era, heavenly teachings, and blessed is the heart which is stirred and attracted by the love of God.*—'Abdu'l-Bahá

(*Selections from the Writings of 'Abdu'l-Bahá*, no. 18.3)

Another important means of becoming informed of someone's character is to examine their relationships with their parents. In many cases, this will provide insight into what kind of spouse or parent they will become, since we frequently model ourselves in the role of parent or spouse after our own parents. Children from happy, stable, unified families have the best preparation for marriage because they have been exposed to good models. They have been affected by what Shoghi Effendi called "the dynamic force of . . . example."*

*The fruits that best befit the tree of human life are trustworthiness and godliness, truthfulness and sincerity;*

---

* Shoghi Effendi, *The Advent of Divine Justice*, ¶47.

*but greater than all, after recognition of the unity of God, praised and glorified be He, is regard for the rights that are due to one's parents. This teaching hath been mentioned in all the Books of God, and reaffirmed by the Most Exalted Pen. Consider that which the Merciful Lord hath revealed in the Qur'án, exalted are His words: "Worship ye God, join with Him no peer or likeness; and show forth kindliness and charity towards your parents . . ." Observe how loving-kindness to one's parents hath been linked to recognition of the one true God!*—Bahá'u'lláh

(*The Kitab-i-Aqdas, Questions and Answers,* no. 106)

*There are also certain sacred duties of children towards parents, which*

*duties are written in the Book of God, as belonging to God. The (children's) prosperity in this world and the Kingdom depends upon the good pleasure of parents, and without this they will be in manifest loss.*
—'Abdu'l-Bahá

(*Lights of Guidance*, no. 505)

*According to the teachings of Bahá'u'lláh the family, being a human unit, must be educated according to the rules of sanctity. All the virtues must be taught the family. The integrity of the family bond must be constantly considered, and the rights of the individual members must not be transgressed. The rights of the son, the father, the mother—none of them must be transgressed, none of them must be arbitrary. Just*

> *as the son has certain obligations to his father, the father, likewise, has certain obligations to his son. The mother, the sister and other members of the household have their certain prerogatives. All these rights and prerogatives must be conserved, yet the unity of the family must be sustained. The injury of one shall be considered the injury of all; the comfort of each, the comfort of all; the honor of one, the honor of all.*
>
> —'Abdu'l-Bahá
>
> (*The Promulgation of Universal Peace*, pp. 232–33)

In summary, a person can, with detachment, evaluate his or her own readiness for marriage and, in the process of becoming informed of another's true character, decide whether or not his or her selection reflects spiritual wisdom. If both persons, in their behavior and relationships with others, reflect those basic virtues prerequisite to a stable marriage, then they will probably manage all the difficulties and adjustments that married life may involve.

Selecting a mate is the prerogative of each person.

> *As for the question regarding marriage under the Law of God: first thou must choose one who is pleasing to thee, and then the matter is subject to the consent of father and mother. Before thou makest thy choice, they have no right to interfere.*
> —'Abdu'l-Bahá
> (*Selections from the Writings of 'Abdu'l-Bahá*, no. 85.1)

If this selection has been made by a loving mind and an informed heart, the likelihood of two souls building a spiritual marriage is high. Furthermore parents will very likely be happy with the selection and give their consent and support to the marriage of two people who are spiritually deepened and socially mature and therefore well-prepared for married life.

— 5 —

# Parental Consent

Once the couple are resolved in their intentions to marry, they must seek consent from all living natural parents. Until this consent is freely given, the marriage cannot take place. The importance of this Bahá'í law can be seen more easily if we understand that marriage is not merely a legalized relationship between a man and a woman, but a social and spiritual contract that involves the extended families of each partner, a contract that has many implications for the welfare of the next generation. The function of this law is to prevent irreparable disunity from occurring within and between families; the unity of mankind must begin with the unity at the family level.

*Show honour to your parents and pay homage to them. This will cause blessings to descend upon you from the clouds of the bounty of your Lord, the Exalted, the Great.*
—Bahá'u'lláh

(*Lights of Guidance*, no. 768)

*Marriage is dependent upon the consent of both parties. Desiring to establish love, unity and harmony amidst Our servants, We have conditioned it, once the couple's wish*

*is known, upon the permission of their parents, lest enmity and rancor should arise amongst them.*
—Bahá'u'lláh

(The Kitáb-i-Aqdas, ¶65)

*The validity of a Bahá'í marriage is dependent upon the free and full consent of all four parents. The freedom of the parents in the exercise of this right is unrestricted and unconditioned. They may refuse their consent on any ground, and they are responsible for their decision to God alone.*
—On behalf of Shoghi Effendi

(*The Compilation of Compilations,* 2:2312)

*Bahá'u'lláh has clearly stated the consent of all living parents is re-*

*quired for a Bahá'í marriage. This applies whether the parents are Bahá'ís or non-Bahá'ís, divorced for years or not. This great law He has laid down to strengthen the social fabric, to knit closer the ties of the home, to place a certain gratitude and respect in the hearts of children for those who have given them life and sent their souls out on the eternal journey towards their Creator. We Bahá'ís must realize that in present-day society the exact opposite process is taking place: young people care less and less for their parents' wishes, divorce is considered a natural right, and obtained on the flimsiest and most unwarrantable and shabby pretexts. People separated from each other, especially if one of them has had full custody of the children, are only too willing to belittle the importance of the part-*

*ner in marriage also responsible as a parent for bringing those children into this world. The Bahá'ís must, through rigid adherence to the Bahá'í laws and teachings, combat these corrosive forces which are so rapidly destroying home life and the beauty of family relationships, and tearing down the moral structure of society.*

—On behalf of Shoghi Effendi

(*The Compilation of Compilations*, 1:544)

*Bahá'u'lláh definitely says that the consent of the parents should be obtained before the marriage is sanctioned and that undoubtedly has great wisdom. It will at least detain young people from marrying without considering the subject thoroughly.*

—On behalf of Shoghi Effendi

(*Lights of Guidance*, no. 1233)

*In many cases of breach of marriage laws the believers apparently look upon the law requiring consent of parents before marriage as a mere administrative regulation, and do not seem to realize that this is a law of great importance affecting the very foundations of human society. Moreover they seem not to appreciate that in the Bahá'í Faith the spiritual and administrative aspects are complementary and that the social laws of the Faith are as binding as the purely spiritual ones.*

—The Universal House of Justice

(*Lights of Guidance*, no. 1236)

Deciding whether or not to give consent is an important responsibility that no parent can afford to treat lightly. Irresponsibility on the part of parents is an injustice to their children and will create disunity in the family. Such irresponsibility may take the form of giving consent when one really believes that the couple should not be married, or withholding consent because of selfish reasons or prejudice. The best guide for parents is the standard of conduct established by Bahá'u'lláh Himself—a standard to be applied to themselves in examining their own motives in arriving at a decision and a standard to be applied to the behavior of the persons seeking consent, as a means of determining maturity and readiness for the responsibilities of marriage.* It is both unreasonable and unrealistic for young

---

* For a general discussion of the Bahá'í standard of conduct, see Shoghi Effendi, *The Advent of Divine Justice,* ¶36–52.

people to expect consent if one or both of the prospective marriage partners is emotionally or spiritually immature and has not demonstrated the capacity to assume the responsibilities involved in establishing a home and caring for children. Whatever the decision of the parents, it is binding.

> *It is perfectly true that Bahá'u'lláh's statement that the consent of all living parents is required for marriage places a grave responsibility on each parent. When the parents are Bahá'ís they should, of course, act objectively in withholding or granting their approval. They cannot evade this responsibility by merely acquiescing in their child's wish, nor should they be swayed by prejudice; but, whether they be Bahá'í or non-Bahá'í, the*

*parents' decision is binding, whatever the reason that may have motivated it. Children must recognize and understand that this act of consenting is the duty of a parent. They must have respect in their hearts for those who have given them life, and whose good pleasure they must at all times strive to win.*

—The Universal House of Justice
(*Lights of Guidance*, no. 1237)

*The responsibilities laid upon parents as they give consideration to the question of consent to marriage of their children is directed to their conscience and therefore it is not possible to apply sanctions. On the other hand, the Bahá'í law requiring children to obtain the consent of their parents to marriage is subject to sanction, and as you know these are matters set forth in the Kitáb-i-Aqdas and in the instructions of the beloved Guardian.*

—The Universal House of Justice

(*Lights of Guidance*, no. 1245)

Since consent is a matter of conscience, a parent is free to change his mind.

*Bahá'u'lláh requires this and makes no provision about a parent changing his or her mind. So they are free to do so. Once the written consent is given and the marriage takes place, the parents have no right to interfere any more.*

—On behalf of Shoghi Effendi

(*Messages to Canada*, pp. 205–6)

At times, when repeated efforts to obtain consent are unsuccessful and conflicts are unresolvable, accepting the outcome can be difficult. But a Bahá'í must realize that he is sacrificing his personal desires so that *"enmity and ill-feeling might be avoided."* *

> *It is surely a very unfortunate case when the parents and children differ on some grave issues of life such as marriage, but the best way is not to flout each other's opinion nor to discuss it in a charged atmosphere but rather try to settle it in an amicable way.*
> —Shoghi Effendi
> (*Bahá'í Marriage and Family Life*, no. 74)

---

* Bahá'u'lláh, Kitáb-i-Aqdas, quoted in J. E. Esslemont, *Bahá'u'lláh and the New Era,* p. 195.

*Obedience to the Laws of Bahá'u'lláh will necessarily impose hardships in individual cases. No one should expect, upon becoming a Bahá'í, that his faith will not be tested, and to our finite understanding of such matters these tests may occasionally seem unbearable. But we are aware of the assurance which Bahá'u'lláh Himself has given the believers that they will never be called upon to meet a test greater than their capacity to endure.*

*It therefore becomes a matter of demonstration of the depth of his faith when he is faced with a divine command the wisdom and rationale of which he cannot at that time understand.*

—The Universal House of Justice

(From a letter dated September 7, 1965,
to a National Spiritual Assembly)

*In considering the effect of obedience to the laws on individual lives, one must remember that the purpose of this life is to prepare the soul for the next. Here one must learn to control and direct one's animal impulses, not to be a slave to them. Life in this world is a succession of tests and achievements, of falling short and of making new spiritual advances. Sometimes the course may seem very hard, but one can witness, again and again, that the soul who steadfastly obeys the law of Bahá'u'lláh, however hard it may seem, grows spiritually, while the one who compromises with the law for the sake of his own apparent happiness is seen to have been following a chimera: he does not attain the happiness he sought, he retards his spiritual ad-*

*vance and often brings new problems upon himself.*

*To give one very obvious example: the Bahá'í law requiring consent of parents to marriage. All too often nowadays such consent is withheld by non-Bahá'í parents for reasons of bigotry or racial prejudice; yet we have seen again and again the profound effect on those very parents of the firmness of the children in the Bahá'í law, to the extent that not only is the consent ultimately given in many cases, but the character of the parents can be affected and their relationship with their child greatly strengthened.*

*Thus, by upholding Bahá'í law in the face of all difficulties we not only strengthen our own characters but influence those around us.*

—The Universal House of Justice

(*Messages from the Universal House of Justice 1968–1973*, pp. 106–7)

*Bahá'ís who cannot marry because of lack of consent of one or more parents could consult with their Local Spiritual Assembly, to see whether it may suggest a way to change the attitude of any of the parents involved. The believers, when faced with such problems, should put their trust in Bahá'u'lláh, devote more time to the service, the teaching and the promotion of His Faith, be absolutely faithful to His injunctions on the observance of an unsullied, chaste life, and rely upon Him to open the way and remove the obstacle, or make known His will.*

—The Universal House of Justice

(*Developing Distinctive Bahá'í Communities*, ch. 12, p. 21)

— 6 —

# The Ceremony

A Bahá'í ceremony, in which the couple recites the verse revealed by Bahá'u'lláh for marriage, is a prerequisite to Bahá'í marriage, whether or not it is recognized as legal by the state.

> *The Bahá'í marriage ceremony should be carried out because we are Bahá'ís, regardless of whether it is legal or not.*
>
> —On behalf of Shoghi Effendi
>
> (From a letter dated July 5, 1950, written to the National Spiritual Assembly of the United States—*Bahá'í News,* no. 236, October 1950, p. 3)

> *Although those married in a civil or religious ceremony before becoming Bahá'ís are accepted as married under Bahá'í law, persons wishing to marry after they become Bahá'ís must have a Bahá'í ceremony and are indeed not regarded as married unless they have met the requirements of Bahá'í law.*
>
> —The Universal House of Justice
>
> (From a letter dated May 22, 1967, to a National Spiritual Assembly)

A Bahá'í ceremony should take place even if one partner is not a Bahá'í:

> *If a Bahá'í marries a non-Bahá'í who wishes to have the religious ceremony of his own sect carried out, it must be quite clear that, first, the*

*Bahá'í partner is understood to be a Bahá'í by religion, and not to accept the religion of the other party to the marriage through having his or her religious ceremony; and second, the ceremony must be of a nature which does not commit the Bahá'í to any declaration of faith in a religion other than his own.*

*Under these circumstances, the Bahá'í can partake of the religious ceremony of his non-Bahá'í partner. The Bahá'í should insist on having the Bahá'í ceremony carried out before or after the non-Bahá'í one, on the same day.*

—On behalf of Shoghi Effendi

(From a letter dated June 20, 1954, written to the National Spiritual Assembly of the United States—*Bahá'í News,* no. 283, September 1954, p. 2)

*With reference to your question regarding mixed marriages, that is to say between Bahá'ís and non-Bahá'ís; in all such cases the believer must insist that the Bahá'í ceremony should, as far as he is concerned, be performed in its entirety, but should also give full freedom to the other contracting party to carry out the non-Bahá'í rite or ceremony be it Muslim, Christian or otherwise, provided the latter does not invalidate the Bahá'í marriage act.*

—On behalf of Shoghi Effendi

(*Lights of Guidance*, no. 1282)

The Bahá'í marriage ceremony is very simple and should remain free of dogma and ritual. There is no set standard for how Bahá'ís must conduct the ceremony. The only requirement is that the Bahá'í marriage vow be recited by both parties in front of two witnesses.

> *Bahá'í marriage should at present not be pressed into any kind of a uniform mold. What is absolutely essential is what Bahá'u'lláh stipulated in the Aqdas: the friends can add to these selected writings if they please.*
> —On behalf of Shoghi Effendi
>
> (From a letter dated October 5, 1946, written to the National Spiritual Assembly of the United States and Canada—*Bahá'í News*, no. 192, February 1947, p. 6)

> *There is no ritual, according to the Aqdas, and the Guardian is very anxious that none should be introduced at present and no general forms accepted. He believes this ceremony should be as simple as possible, the parties using the words ordained*

*by Bahá'u'lláh, and excerpts from the writings and prayers being read if desired. There should be no commingling of the old forms with the new and simple one of Bahá'u'lláh, and Bahá'ís should not be married in the Church or any other acknowledged place of worship of the followers of other Faiths.*

—On behalf of Shoghi Effendi

(*Lights of Guidance*, no. 1298)

*The bride and groom, before two witnesses, must state 'We will all, verily, abide by the Will of God.' These two witnesses may be chosen by the couple or by the Spiritual Assembly, but must in any case be acceptable to the Assembly; they may be its chairman and secretary, or two other members of the Assembly, or two other people, Bahá'í or non-Bahá'í, or any combination of these. The Assembly may decide that all marriage certificates it issues are to be signed by the chairman and secretary, but that is a different matter and has nothing to do with the actual ceremony or the witnesses.*

*. . . The witnesses can be any two trustworthy people whose testimony is acceptable to the Spiritual Assembly under whose jurisdiction the marriage is performed. This fact makes it possible for a lone pioneer in a remote post to have a Bahá'í marriage.*

—The Universal House of Justice

(From a letter dated August 8, 1969, to a National Spiritual Assembly)

*When a Bahá'í marriage ceremony takes place, there is no individual, strictly speaking, who 'performs' it—no Bahá'í equivalent to a minister of the Church. The couple themselves perform the ceremony by each saying, in the presence of at least two witnesses, the prescribed verse "We will all, verily, abide by the Will of God." This ceremony is performed under the authority of a Spiritual Assembly which has the responsibility for ensuring that the various requirements of Bahá'í law, such as obtaining the consent of the parents, are met, to whom the witnesses must be acceptable, and which issues the marriage certificate.*

*The sincerity with which the sacred verse is spoken is a matter for the consciences of those who utter it.*

*According to the explicit text of the Kitáb-i-Aqdas, both the bride and groom must, in the presence of witnesses, recite the prescribed verse; this is an essential requirement of the marriage ceremony. Thus if a Bahá'í is marrying a non-Bahá'í and this person for any reason refuses to utter this verse, then the Bahá'í cannot marry that person.*

—On behalf of the Universal House of Justice

(*Lights of Guidance*, no. 1284)

*In response to your email . . . we have been instructed by the Universal House of Justice to send you the following clarifications:*

*–When two Bahá'ís are marrying, the wedding ceremony should not be held in the place*

*of worship of another religion, nor should the forms of the marriage of other religions be added to the simple Bahá'í ceremony.*

*–When a Bahá'í is marrying a non-Bahá'í, and the religious wedding ceremony of the non-Bahá'í partner is to be held in addition to the Bahá'í ceremony, both ceremonies may, if requested, be held in the place of worship of the other religion provided that:*

*–Equal respect is accorded to both ceremonies. In other words, the Bahá'í ceremony, which is basically so simple, should not be regarded as a mere formal adjunct to the ceremony of the other religion.*

*–The two ceremonies are clearly distinct. In other words, they should not be commingled into one combined ceremony.*
—On behalf of the Universal House of Justice
(*Lights of Guidance*, no. 1295)

— 7 —

# Interracial Marriage

Consistent with the principle of the essential oneness of humanity and the belief that our purpose in life is to promote that oneness, interracial marriage is encouraged. In fact, it is advocated as a powerful means by which racial unity in the world can be achieved.

*O Children of Men! Know ye not why We created you all from the same dust? That no one should exalt himself over the other. Ponder at all times in your hearts how ye were created. Since We have created you all from one same substance it is incumbent on you to be even as one soul, to walk with the same feet, eat with the same mouth and dwell in the same land, that from your inmost being, by your deeds and actions, the signs of oneness and the essence of detachment may be made manifest. Such is My counsel to you, O concourse of light! Heed ye this counsel that ye may obtain the fruit of holiness from the tree of wondrous glory.*

—Bahá'u'lláh

(Hidden Words, Arabic, no. 68)

*O well-beloved ones! The tabernacle of unity hath been raised; regard ye not one another as strangers. Ye are the fruits of one tree, and the leaves of one branch.*—Bahá'u'lláh

(*Gleanings from the Writings of Bahá'u'lláh*, no. 112.1)

*Numerous points of partnership and agreement exist between the two races; whereas the one point of distinction is that of color. Shall this, the least of all distinctions, be allowed to separate you as races and individuals? . . .*

*But there is need of a superior power to overcome human prejudices, a power which nothing in the world of mankind can withstand and which will overshadow the effect of all other forces at work in human conditions. That irresistible power is the love of God. It is my hope and prayer that it may destroy the prejudice of this one point of distinction between you and unite you all permanently under its hallowed protection. Bahá'u'lláh has proclaimed the oneness of the world of humanity. He has caused various nations and divergent creeds to unite. He has declared that difference of race and color is like the variegated beauty of flowers in a garden. If you enter a garden, you will see yellow, white, blue, red flowers in profusion and beauty—each radiant within itself and although different from the others, lending its own charm to them. Racial difference in the human kingdom is similar. If all the flowers in a garden were of the same color, the effect would be monotonous and wearying to the eye.*

*Therefore, Bahá'u'lláh hath said that the various races of human-*

*kind lend a composite harmony and beauty of color to the whole. Let all associate, therefore, in this great human garden even as flowers grow and blend together side by side without discord or disagreement between them.*—'Abdu'l-Bahá

(*The Promulgation of Universal Peace*, pp. 93–94)

*When perfect justice reigns in every country of the Eastern and Western World, then will the earth become a place of beauty. The dignity and equality of every servant of God will be acknowledged; the ideal of the solidarity of the human race, the true brotherhood of man, will be realized; and the glorious light of the Sun of Truth will illumine the souls of all men.*—'Abdu'l-Bahá

(*Paris Talks*, no. 47.6)

*Work and pray for the unity of mankind, that all the races of the earth may become one race, all the countries one country, and that all hearts may beat as one heart, working together for perfect unity and brotherhood.*—'Abdu'l-Bahá

(*Paris Talks*, no. 32.3)

*One of the great principles of Bahá'u'lláh's teachings is the establishment of agreement among the peoples of the world. . . . He proclaimed international unity, summoned the religions of the world to harmony and reconciliation and established fellowship among many races, sects and communities.*

—'Abdu'l-Bahá

(*The Promulgation of Universal Peace*, p. 547)

*Your statement to the effect that the principle of oneness of mankind prevents any true Bahá'í from regarding race itself as a bar to union is in complete accord with the Teachings of the Faith on this point. For both Bahá'u'lláh and 'Abdu'l-Bahá never disapproved of the idea of interracial marriage, nor discouraged it. The Bahá'í Teachings, indeed, by their very nature transcend all limitations imposed by race, and as such can and should never be identified with any particular school of racial philosophy.*

—On behalf of Shoghi Effendi

(*Lights of Guidance*, no. 1288)

— 8 —

# Prayers for Marriage

Prayer is a powerful means of maintaining the spiritual foundation of marriage. It strengthens one's commitment to the vow to abide by God's will made during the ceremony and supports our efforts to reflect God's purpose for humanity.

*Reflect awhile, and consider how they who are the loved ones of God must conduct themselves, and to what heights they must soar. Beseech thou, at all times, thy Lord, the God of Mercy, to aid them to do what He willeth. He, verily, is the Most Powerful, the All-Glorious, the All-Knowing.*—Bahá'u'lláh

(*Gleanings from the Writings of Bahá'u'lláh*, no. 115.8)

*Praise be to God, thy heart is engaged in the commemoration of God, thy soul is gladdened by the glad tidings of God and thou art absorbed in prayer. The state of prayer is the best of conditions, for man is then associating with God. Prayer verily bestoweth life, particularly when offered in private and at times, such as midnight, when freed from daily cares.*—'Abdu'l-Bahá

(*Selections from the Writings of 'Abdu'l-Bahá*, no. 172.1)

While the rich treasury of prayers bequeathed to us by Bahá'u'lláh and 'Abdu'l-Bahá is a source of light and assistance for many aspects of our lives, special prayers for marriage were also revealed.

*He is the Bestower, the Bounteous!*

*Praise be to God, the Ancient, the Ever-Abiding, the Changeless, the Eternal! He Who hath testified in His Own Being that verily He is the One, the Single, the Untrammeled, the Exalted. We bear witness that verily there is no God but Him, acknowledging His oneness, confessing His singleness. He hath ever dwelt in unapproachable heights, in the summits of His loftiness, sanctified from the mention of aught save Himself, free from the description of aught but Him.*

*And when He desired to manifest grace and beneficence to men, and to set the world in order, He revealed observances and created laws; among them He established the law of marriage, made it as a fortress for well-being and salvation, and enjoined it upon us in that which was sent down out of the heaven of sanctity in His Most Holy Book. He saith, great is His glory: "Enter into wedlock, O people, that ye may bring forth one who will make mention of Me amid My servants. This is My bidding unto you; hold fast to it as an assistance to yourselves."*—Bahá'u'lláh

(*Bahá'í Prayers*, pp. 117–18)

*He is God!*

*O peerless Lord! In Thine almighty wisdom Thou hast enjoined*

*marriage upon the peoples, that the generations of men may succeed one another in this contingent world, and that ever, so long as the world shall last, they may busy themselves at the Threshold of Thy oneness with servitude and worship, with salutation, adoration and praise. "I have not created spirits and men, but that they should worship me."* Wherefore, wed Thou in the heaven of Thy mercy these two birds of the nest of Thy love, and make them the means of attracting perpetual grace; that from the union of these two seas of love a wave of tenderness may surge and cast the pearls of pure and goodly issue on the shore of*

* Qur'án 51:56.

*life. "He hath let loose the two seas, that they meet each other: Between them is a barrier which they overpass not. Which then of the bounties of your Lord will ye deny? From each He bringeth up greater and lesser pearls."**

*O Thou kind Lord! Make Thou this marriage to bring forth coral and pearls. Thou art verily the All-Powerful, the Most Great, the Ever-Forgiving.*—'Abdu'l-Bahá

(*Bahá'í Prayers*, pp. 118–20)

*Glory be unto Thee, O my God! Verily, this Thy servant and this Thy maidservant have gathered under the shadow of Thy mercy and they are united through Thy favor and*

* Qur'án 55:19–20.

*generosity. O Lord! Assist them in this Thy world and Thy kingdom and destine for them every good through Thy bounty and grace. O Lord! Confirm them in Thy servitude and assist them in Thy service. Suffer them to become the signs of Thy Name in Thy world and protect them through Thy bestowals which are inexhaustible in this world and the world to come. O Lord! They are supplicating the kingdom of Thy mercifulness and invoking the realm of Thy singleness. Verily, they are married in obedience to Thy command. Cause them to become the signs of harmony and unity until the end of time. Verily, Thou art the Omnipotent, the Omnipresent and the Almighty!*—'Abdu'l-Bahá

(*Bahá'í Prayers*, p. 120)

*O my Lord, O my Lord! These two bright orbs are wedded in Thy love, conjoined in servitude to Thy Holy Threshold, united in ministering to Thy Cause. Make Thou this marriage to be as threading lights of Thine abounding grace, O my Lord, the All-Merciful, and luminous rays of Thy bestowals, O Thou the Beneficent, the Ever-Giving, that there may branch out from this great tree boughs that will grow green and flourishing through the gifts that rain down from Thy clouds of grace.*

*Verily, Thou art the Generous. Verily, Thou art the Almighty. Verily, Thou art the Compassionate, the All-Merciful.*

—'Abdu'l-Bahá

(*Bahá'í Prayers*, p. 121)

In addition to special prayers for marriage, Bahá'u'lláh and 'Abdu'l-Bahá have also revealed many prayers that strengthen our determination to abide by the will of God.

> *O my God! O my God! Unite the hearts of Thy servants, and reveal to them Thy great purpose. May they follow Thy commandments and abide in Thy law. Help them, O God, in their endeavor, and grant them strength to serve Thee. O God! Leave them not to themselves, but guide their steps by the light of Thy knowledge, and cheer their hearts by Thy love. Verily, Thou art their Helper and their Lord.*
>
> —Bahá'u'lláh

(*Bahá'í Prayers*, p. 238)

*I give praise to Thee, O my God, that the fragrance of Thy loving-kindness hath enraptured me, and the gentle winds of Thy mercy have inclined me in the direction of Thy bountiful favors. Make me to quaff, O my Lord, from the fingers of Thy bounteousness the living waters which have enabled every one that hath partaken of them to rid himself of all attachment to any one save Thee, and to soar into the atmosphere of detachment from all Thy creatures, and to fix his gaze upon Thy loving providence and Thy manifold gifts.*

*Make me ready, in all circumstances, O my Lord, to serve Thee and to set myself towards the adored sanctuary of Thy Revelation and of Thy Beauty. If it be Thy pleasure, make me to grow as a tender herb in the meadows of Thy grace, that the gentle winds of Thy will may stir me up and bend me into conformity with Thy pleasure, in such wise that my movement and my stillness may be wholly directed by Thee.*

*Thou art He, by Whose name the Hidden Secret was divulged, and the Well-Guarded Name was revealed, and the seals of the sealed-up Goblet were opened, shedding thereby its fragrance over all creation, whether of the past or of the future. He who was athirst, O my Lord, hath hasted to attain the living waters of Thy grace, and the wretched creature hath yearned to immerse himself beneath the ocean of Thy riches.*

*I swear by Thy glory, O Lord the Beloved of the world and the Desire of all them that have recognized*

*Thee! I am sore afflicted by the grief of my separation from Thee, in the days when the Day-Star of Thy presence hath shed its radiance upon Thy people. Write down, then, for me the recompense decreed for such as have gazed on Thy face, and have, by Thy leave, gained admittance into the court of Thy throne, and have, at Thy bidding, met Thee face to face.*

*I implore Thee, O my Lord, by Thy name the splendors of which have encompassed the earth and the heavens, to enable me so to surrender my will to what Thou hast decreed in Thy Tablets, that I may cease to discover within me any desire except what Thou didst desire through the power of Thy sovereignty, and any will save what Thou didst destine for me by Thy will.*

*Whither shall I turn, O my God, powerless as I am to discover any other way except the way Thou didst set before Thy chosen Ones? All the atoms of the earth proclaim Thee to be God, and testify that there is none other God besides Thee. Thou hast from eternity been powerful to do what Thou hast willed, and to ordain what Thou hast pleased.*

*Do Thou destine for me, O my God, what will set me, at all times, towards Thee, and enable me to cleave continually to the cord of Thy grace, and to proclaim Thy name, and to look for whatsoever may flow down from Thy pen. I am poor and desolate, O my Lord, and Thou art the All-Possessing, the Most High. Have pity, then, upon me through the wonders of Thy mercy, and send down upon me, every moment of my life, the things wherewith Thou hast recreated the hearts of all Thy creatures who have recognized Thy unity, and of all Thy people who are wholly devoted to Thee.*

*Thou, verily, art the Almighty, the Most Exalted, the All-Knowing, the All-Wise.*—Bahá'u'lláh

(*Prayers and Meditations*, pp. 240–42)

*All praise be to Thee, O my God, for the things Thou didst ordain for me through Thy decree and by the power of Thy sovereignty. I beseech Thee that Thou wilt fortify both myself and them that love me in our love for Thee, and wilt keep us firm in Thy Cause. I swear by Thy might! O my God! Thy servant's shame is to be shut out as by a veil from Thee, and his glory is to know Thee. Armed with the power of Thy name nothing can ever hurt me, and with Thy love in my heart all the world's afflictions can in no wise alarm me.*

*Send down, therefore, O my Lord, upon me and upon my loved ones that which will protect us from the mischief of those that have repudiated Thy truth and disbelieved in Thy signs.*

*Thou art, verily, the All-Glorious, the Most Bountiful.*—Bahá'u'lláh

(*Prayers and Meditations by Bahá'u'lláh*, p. 208)

*Make firm our steps, O Lord, in Thy path and strengthen Thou our hearts in Thine obedience. Turn our faces toward the beauty of Thy oneness, and gladden our bosoms with the*

*signs of Thy divine unity. Adorn our bodies with the robe of Thy bounty, and remove from our eyes the veil of sinfulness, and give us the chalice of Thy grace; that the essence of all beings may sing Thy praise before the vision of Thy grandeur. Reveal then Thyself, O Lord, by Thy merciful utterance and the mystery of Thy divine being, that the holy ecstasy of prayer may fill our souls—a prayer that shall rise above words and letters and transcend the murmur of syllables and sounds—that all things may be merged into nothingness before the revelation of Thy splendor.*

*Lord! These are servants that have remained fast and firm in Thy Covenant and Thy Testament, that have held fast unto the cord of constancy in Thy Cause and clung unto the hem of the robe of Thy grandeur. Assist them, O Lord, with Thy grace, confirm them with Thy power and strengthen their loins in obedience to Thee.*

*Thou art the Pardoner, the Gracious.*

—'Abdu'l-Bahá

(*Bahá'í Prayers*, pp. 69–70)

*O Lord my God! Assist Thy loved ones to be firm in Thy Faith, to walk in Thy ways, to be steadfast in Thy Cause. Give them Thy grace to withstand the onslaught of self and passion, to follow the light of divine guidance. Thou art the Powerful, the Gracious, the Self-Subsisting, the Bestower, the Compassionate, the Almighty, the All-Bountiful.*

—'Abdu'l-Bahá

(*Bahá'í Prayers*, p. 191)

Many prayers were also revealed to support and reinforce the strength and unity of the family.

## PRAYER FOR THE FAMILY

*Glory be unto Thee, O Lord my God! I beg Thee to forgive me and those who support Thy Faith. Verily, Thou art the sovereign Lord, the Forgiver, the Most Generous. O my God! Enable such servants of Thine as are deprived of knowledge to be admitted into Thy Cause; for once they learn of Thee, they bear witness to the truth of the Day of Judgment and do not dispute the revelations of Thy bounty. Send down upon them the tokens of Thy grace, and grant them, wherever they reside, a liberal share of that which Thou hast ordained for the pious among Thy servants. Thou art in truth the Supreme Ruler, the All-Bounteous, the Most Benevolent.*

*O my God! Let the outpourings of Thy bounty and blessings descend upon homes whose inmates have embraced Thy Faith, as a token of Thy grace and as a mark of loving-kindness from Thy presence. Verily, unsurpassed art Thou in granting forgiveness. Should Thy bounty be withheld from anyone, how could he be reckoned among the followers of the Faith in Thy Day?*

*Bless me, O my God, and those who will believe in Thy signs on the appointed Day, and such as cherish my love in their hearts—a love which Thou dost instill into Them.*

*Verily, Thou art the Lord of righteousness, the Most Exalted.*
—The Bab

(*Bahá'í Prayers*, pp. 62–63)

## PRAYER FOR HUSBANDS

*O God, my God! This Thy handmaid is calling upon Thee, trusting in Thee, turning her face unto Thee, imploring Thee to shed Thy heavenly bounties upon her, and to disclose unto her Thy spiritual mysteries, and to cast upon her the lights of Thy Godhead.*

*O my Lord! Make the eyes of my husband to see. Rejoice Thou his heart with the light of the knowledge of Thee, draw Thou his mind unto Thy luminous beauty, cheer Thou his spirit by revealing unto him Thy manifest splendors.*

*O my Lord! Lift Thou the veil from before his sight. Rain down Thy plenteous bounties upon him, intoxicate him with the wine of love for Thee, make him one of Thy angels whose feet walk upon this earth even as their souls are soaring through the high heavens. Cause him to become a brilliant lamp, shining out with the light of Thy wisdom in the midst of Thy people.*

*Verily, Thou art the Precious, the Ever-Bestowing, the Open of Hand.*—'Abdu'l-Bahá

(*Bahá'í Prayers*, pp. 64–65)

## PRAYERS FOR PARENTS

*I beg Thy forgiveness, O my God, and implore pardon after the manner Thou wishest Thy servants to di-*

*rect themselves to Thee. I beg of Thee to wash away our sins as befitteth Thy Lordship, and to forgive me, my parents, and those who in Thy estimation have entered the abode of Thy love in a manner which is worthy of Thy transcendent sovereignty and well beseemeth the glory of Thy celestial power.*

*O my God! Thou hast inspired my soul to offer its supplication to Thee, and but for Thee, I would not call upon Thee. Lauded and glorified art Thou; I yield Thee praise inasmuch as Thou didst reveal Thyself unto me, and I beg Thee to forgive me, since I have fallen short in my duty to know Thee and have failed to walk in the path of Thy love.*—The Bab

(*Bahá'í Prayers*, p. 63-4)

*O Lord! In this Most Great Dispensation Thou dost accept the intercession of children in behalf of their parents. This is one of the special infinite bestowals of this Dispensation. Therefore, O Thou kind Lord, accept the request of this Thy servant at the threshold of Thy singleness and submerge his father in the ocean of Thy grace, because this son hath arisen to render Thee service and is exerting effort at all times in the pathway of Thy love, Verily, Thou art the Giver, the Forgiver and the Kind!*—'Abdu'l-Bahá

(*Bahá'í Prayers*, p. 64)

## PRAYER FOR EXPECTANT MOTHERS

*My Lord! My Lord! I praise Thee and I thank Thee for that whereby Thou hast favored Thine humble maidservant, Thy slave beseeching and supplicating Thee, because Thou hast verily guided her unto Thine obvious Kingdom and caused her to hear thine exalted Call in the contingent world and to behold thy Signs which prove the appearance of Thy victorious reign over all things.*

*O my Lord, I dedicate that which is in my womb unto Thee. Then cause it to be a praiseworthy child in Thy Kingdom and a fortunate one by Thy favor and Thy generosity; to develop and to grow up under the charge of Thine education. Verily,*

*Thou art the Gracious! Verily, Thou art the Lord of Great Favor!*

—'Abdu'l-Bahá

(*Bahá'í Prayers*, pp. 249–50)

## PRAYERS FOR INFANTS

*Praised be Thou, O Lord my God! Graciously grant that this infant be fed from the breast of Thy tender mercy and loving providence and be nourished with the fruit of Thy celestial trees. Suffer him not to be committed to the care of anyone save Thee, inasmuch as Thou, Thyself, through the potency of thy sovereign will and power, didst create and call him into being. There is none other God but Thee, the Almighty, the All-Knowing.*

*Lauded art Thou, O my Best Beloved, waft over him the sweet savors of Thy transcendent bounty and the fragrances of Thy holy bestowals. Enable him then to seek shelter beneath the shadow of Thy most exalted Name, O Thou Who holdest in Thy grasp the kingdom of names and attributes. Verily, Thou art potent to do what Thou willest, and Thou art indeed the Mighty, the Exalted, the Ever-Forgiving, the Gracious, the Generous, the Merciful.*—Bahá'u'lláh

(*Bahá'í Prayers*, pp. 32–33)

*O Thou peerless Lord! Let this suckling babe be nursed from the breast of Thy loving-kindness, guard it within the cradle of Thy safety and protection and grant that it be*

*reared in the arms of Thy tender affection.*—'Abdu'l-Bahá

(*Bahá'í Prayers*, p. 33)

*O God! Rear this little babe in the bosom of Thy love, and give it milk from the breast of Thy Providence. Cultivate this fresh plant in the rose garden of Thy love and aid it to grow through the showers of Thy bounty. Make it a child of the kingdom, and lead it to Thy heavenly realm. Thou art powerful and kind, and Thou art the Bestower, the Generous, the Lord of surpassing bounty.*
—'Abdu'l-Bahá

(*Bahá'í Prayers*, pp. 33–34)

## PRAYERS FOR CHILDREN

*O God! Educate these children. These children are the plants of*

*Thine orchard, the flowers of Thy meadow, the roses of Thy garden. Let Thy rain fall upon them; let the Sun of Reality shine upon them with Thy love. Let Thy breeze refresh them in order that they may be trained, grow and develop, and appear in the utmost beauty. Thou art the Giver. Thou art the Compassionate.*

—'Abdu'l-Bahá

(*Bahá'í Prayers*, p. 28)

*O Thou kind Lord! These lovely children are the handiwork of the fingers of Thy might and the wondrous signs of Thy greatness. O God! Protect these children, graciously assist them to be educated and enable them to render service to the world of humanity. O God! These children are pearls, cause them to be nurtured within the shell of Thy loving-kindness.*

*Thou art the Bountiful, the All-Loving.*—'Abdu'l-Bahá

(*Bahá'í Prayers*, p. 28)

*O Lord! Make these children excellent plants. Let them grow and develop in the Garden of Thy Covenant, and bestow freshness and beauty through the outpourings of the clouds of the all-glorious Kingdom.*

*O Thou kind Lord! I am a little child, exalt me by admitting me to the kingdom. I am earthly, make me heavenly; I am of the world below, let me belong to the realm above; gloomy, suffer me to become radiant; material, make me spiritual, and grant that I may manifest Thine infinite bounties.*

*Thou art the Powerful, the All-Loving.*—'Abdu'l-Bahá

(*Bahá'í Prayers*, pp. 28–29)

*O my Lord! O my Lord!*

*I am a child of tender years. Nourish me from the breast of Thy mercy, train me in the bosom of Thy love, educate me in the school of Thy guidance and develop me under the shadow of Thy bounty. Deliver me from darkness, make me a brilliant light; free me from unhappiness, make me a flower of the rose garden; suffer me to become a servant of Thy threshold and confer upon me the disposition and nature of the righteous; make me a cause of bounty to the human world, and crown my head with the diadem of eternal life.*

*Verily, Thou art the Powerful, the Mighty, the Seer, the Hearer.*

—'Abdu'l-Bahá

(*Bahá'í Prayers*, pp. 29–30)

*O Peerless Lord! Be Thou a shelter for this poor child and a kind and forgiving Master unto this erring and unhappy soul. O Lord! Though we are but worthless plants, yet we belong to Thy garden of roses. Though saplings without leaves and blossoms, yet we are a part of Thine orchard. Nurture this plant then through the outpourings of the clouds of Thy tender mercy and quicken and refresh this sapling through the reviving breath of Thy spiritual spring-*

*time. Suffer him to become heedful, discerning and noble, and grant that he may attain eternal life and abide in Thy Kingdom for evermore.*
—'Abdu'l-Bahá

(*Bahá'í Prayers*, pp. 30–31)

*O Lord! Make this youth radiant, and confer Thy bounty upon this poor creature. Bestow upon him knowledge, grant him added strength at the break of every morn and guard him within the shelter of Thy protection so that he may be freed from error, may devote himself to the service of Thy Cause, may guide the wayward, lead the hapless, free the captives and awaken the heedless, that all may be blessed with Thy remembrance and praise. Thou art the Mighty and the Powerful.*—'Abdu'l-Bahá

(*Bahá'í Prayers*, p. 254)

*O Thou most glorious Lord! Make this little maidservant of Thine blessed and happy; cause her to be cherished at the threshold of Thy oneness and let her drink deep from the cup of Thy love so that she may be filled with rapture and ecstasy and diffuse sweet-scented fragrance. Thou art the Mighty and the Powerful, and Thou art the All- Knowing, the All-Seeing.*—'Abdu'l-Bahá

(*Bahá'í Prayers*, p. 32)

# Part III

# BUILDING A FORTRESS FOR WELL-BEING

— 9 —

# Building and Maintaining the Fortress

Bahá'u'lláh's description of marriage as *"a fortress for well-being and salvation"* conveys a sense of abiding security, safety, and spiritual happiness. It is, however, a fortress that has to be built by the marriage partners themselves, with the assistance of their families, their communities, and Bahá'í institutions. The only solid foundation for this fortress is an understanding of marriage in light of God's purpose for humanity, as presented in Part I, and a good preparation for marriage, as discussed in Part II.

Yet it is unrealistic to think that it would be possible for every prospective married couple to attain a perfect understanding of Bahá'í marriage and have a fully adequate preparation for it. Furthermore, many people are already married when they become Bahá'ís and want to begin building that *"fortress for well-being"* in accordance with Bahá'u'lláh's teachings, no matter what the status of their marriage was prior to their becoming followers of Bahá'u'lláh. In any case, a couple at whatever stage they may find themselves in building their *"fortress for well-being"* will understand that there are always difficulties to face and tests to overcome (as well as joys to be grateful for) if the marital union is to grow in strength and spirituality.

Because we live in an age of transition—an age that is witnessing the rolling up of the old world order—it would be unreasonable to expect that Bahá'í marriages and the quality of Bahá'í family life would be completely unaffected by the influences and pressures of that old order that, if we allow them to, will inevitably undermine the stability of the fortress we are trying to build. The more immature we are spiritually, the more vulnerable we are to these influences and the more efforts we have to make to remain steadfast in our determination to continue building our *"fortress for well-being and salvation."* Couples should expect to encounter tests and difficulties during their marriage, but by relying on

God they will be able to overcome whatever hardships arise.

> *The mind and spirit of man advance when he is tried by suffering. The more the ground is ploughed the better the seed will grow, the better the harvest will be. Just as the plough furrows the earth deeply, purifying it of weeds and thistles, so suffering and tribulation free man from the petty affairs of this worldly life until he arrives at a state of complete detachment. His attitude in this world will be that of divine happiness. Man is, so to speak, unripe: the heat of the fire of suffering will mature him. Look back to the times past and you will find that the greatest men have suffered most.*—'Abdu'l-Bahá
>
> (*Paris Talks*, no. 57.1)

*While a man is happy he may forget his God; but when grief comes and sorrows overwhelm him, then will he remember his Father who is in Heaven, and who is able to deliver him from his humiliations.*

*Men who suffer not, attain no perfection. The plant most pruned by the gardeners is that one which, when the summer comes, will have the most beautiful blossoms and the most abundant fruit.*

—'Abdu'l-Bahá

(*Paris Talks*, no. 14.8–9)

*Naturally there will be periods of distress and difficulty, and even severe tests; but if that person turns firmly toward the Divine Manifestation, studies carefully His Spiritual teachings and receives the blessings of the*

*Holy Spirit, he will find that in reality these tests and difficulties have been the gifts of God to enable him to grow and develop.*
—On behalf of Shoghi Effendi
(*Lights of Guidance*, no. 247)

*As long as there will be life on earth, there will be also suffering, in various forms and degrees. But suffering, although an inescapable reality, can nevertheless be utilised as a means for the attainment of happiness. This is the interpretation given to it by all the prophets and saints who, in the midst of severe tests and trials, felt happy and joyous and experienced what is best and holiest in life. Suffering is both a reminder and a guide. It stimulates us to better adapt ourselves to our environmental con-*

*ditions, and thus leads the way to self-improvement. In every suffering one can find a meaning and a wisdom. But it is not always easy to find the secret of that wisdom. It is sometimes only when all our suffering has passed that we become aware of its usefulness. What man considers to be evil turns often to be a cause of infinite blessings. And this is due to his desire to know more than he can. God's wisdom is, indeed, inscrutable to us all, and it is no use pushing too far trying to discover that which shall always remain a mystery to our mind.*

—On behalf of Shoghi Effendi

(*Lights of Guidance*, no. 944)

*You should rest assured that your strict adherence to the laws and ob-*

> *servances enjoined by Bahá'u'lláh is the one power that can effectively guide and enable you to overcome the tests and trials of your life, and help you to continually grow and develop spiritually.*
>
> —On behalf of Shoghi Effendi
>
> (*The Compilation of Compilations*, 2:1769)

Yet in spite of the challenges we may encounter in society or within marriage, every marriage is a union that has the potential to become truly divine in nature.

> *The love between husband and wife should not be purely physical, nay rather it must be spiritual and heavenly. These two souls should be considered as one soul. How difficult*

*it would be to divide a single soul! Nay, great would be the difficulty!*

*The foundation of the kingdom of God is based upon harmony and love, oneness, relationship and union, not upon differences, especially between husband and wife.* . . . —'Abdu'l-Bahá

(*Lights of Guidance*, no. 1306)

*The life of a married couple should resemble the life of the angels in heaven—a life full of joy and spiritual delight, a life of unity and concord, a friendship both mental and physical. The home should be orderly and well-organized. Their ideas and thoughts should be like the rays of the sun of truth and the radiance of the brilliant stars in the heavens. Even as two birds they should warble mel-*

*odies upon the branches of the tree of fellowship and harmony. They should always be elated with joy and gladness and be a source of happiness to the hearts of others. They should set an example to their fellow-men, manifest true and sincere love towards each other and educate their children in such a manner as to blazon the fame and glory of their family.*—'Abdu'l-Bahá

(*Lights of Guidance*, no. 733)

*Wherefore must the friends of God, with utter sanctity, with one accord, rise up in the spirit, in unity with one another, to such a degree that they will become even as one being and one soul. On such a plane as this, physical bodies play no part, rather doth the spirit take over and*

*rule; and when its power encompasseth all then is spiritual union achieved. Strive ye by day and night to cultivate your unity to the fullest degree. Let your thoughts dwell on your own spiritual development, and close your eyes to the deficiencies of other souls. Act ye in such wise, showing forth pure and goodly deeds, and modesty and humility, that ye will cause others to be awakened.*
—'Abdu'l-Bahá

(*Selections from the Writings of 'Abdu'l-Bahá*, no. 174.5)

*A marriage between two souls, alive to the Message of God in this day, dedicated to the service of His Cause, working for the good humanity, can be a potent force in the lives of others and an example and inspiration to other Bahá'ís, as well as to non-believers.*

—On behalf of Shoghi Effendi

(*Lights of Guidance*, no. 1265)

By establishing a happy and loving marriage, a couple can also make their home a reflection of these heavenly attributes.

*My home is the home of peace. My home is the home of joy and delight. My home is the home of laughter and exultation. Whosoever enters through the portals of this home, must go out with gladsome heart. This is the home of light; whosoever enters here must become illumined.*

—'Abdu'l-Bahá

(*The Compilation of Compilations*, 1:859)

*This is in truth a Bahá'í house. Every time such a house or meeting place is founded it becomes one of the greatest aids to the general development of the town and country to which it belongs. It encourages the growth of learning and science and is known for its intense spirituality and for the love it spreads among the peoples.*
—'Abdu'l-Bahá

(*Paris Talks*, no. 24.1)

*It is one of the essential teachings of the Faith that unity should be maintained in the home.*
—On behalf of Shoghi Effendi

(*The Compilation of Compilations*, 2:2156)

*People who come so close to our doors and perhaps enter our home should not be left to go without carrying away some of the delights we are enjoying. They are also seeking souls earnestly desiring to attain their spiritual and social ideals.*

—On behalf of Shoghi Effendi

(*The Compilation of Compilations,* 2:2248)

— 10 —

# Unity: The Strength of the Fortress

Without unity, the fortress upon which the marriage is built will crumble. Unity rests upon an agreement between the marriage partners on fundamentals, such as a mutual understanding of the purpose of life, values and attitudes related to that purpose, and their capacity to appreciate diversity as a source of creativity for the marriage and the home. Both this basic agreement on the purpose of life and the capacity to appreciate diversity begin with submission to the will of God, as expressed in the Bahá'í wedding vow. Submission to God's will, as articulated by Bahá'u'lláh for this age, provides a basis for agreement between marriage partners on fundamental values, enabling them to apprehend God's purpose for humanity and giving them a common source of meaning in their lives. Sharing this common source of meaning generates a fundamental harmony between marriage partners, which in turn can help make it easier for them to appreciate those diversities that bring vitality to unity. The differences that exist between us are a reflection of God's creation, and our unique attributes and qualities should be embraced as contributing to the diversity of the human race, as well as to the marriage union in particular.

> *When divers shades of thought, temperament and character, are brought together under the power and influence of one central agency, the beauty and glory of human perfection will be revealed and made manifest. Naught but the celestial potency of the Word of God, which ruleth and transcendeth the realities of all things, is capable of harmonizing the divergent thoughts, sentiments, ideas and convictions of the children of men.*
> —'Abdu'l-Bahá
>
> (Quoted in *The World Order of Bahá'u'lláh*, p. 42)

*Differences and dissensions, which destroy the foundations of the world of humanity and are contrary to the will and good pleasure of God, disappear completely in the light of the revelation of Bahá'u'lláh; difficult problems are solved, unity and love are established.*—'Abdu'l-Bahá

(*The Promulgation of Universal Peace*, p. 446)

*It is clear that the reality of mankind is diverse, that opinions are various and sentiments different; and this difference of opinions, of thoughts, of intelligence, of sentiments among the human species arises from essential necessity; for the differences in the degrees of existence of creatures is one of the necessities of existence, which unfolds itself in infinite forms. Therefore, we have need of a general power which may*

*dominate the sentiments, the opinions and the thoughts of all, thanks to which these divisions may no longer have effect, and all individuals may be brought under the influence of the unity of the world of humanity. It is clear and evident that this greatest power in the human world is the love of God. It brings the different peoples under the shadow of the tent of affection; it gives to the antagonistic and hostile nations and families the greatest love and union.*
—'Abdu'l-Bahá

(*Some Answered Questions*, p. 301)

This unity, the foundation of the fortress, is strengthened by our attempt to develop our virtues, or attributes of God, which it is our purpose in life to acquire. It is therefore extremely important that both marriage partners encourage and support in loving ways the development of virtues in each other.

> *We must strive with energies of heart, soul and mind to develop and manifest the perfections and virtues latent within the realities of the phenomenal world, for the human reality may be compared to a seed. If we sow the seed, a mighty tree appears from it. The virtues of the seed are revealed in the tree; it puts forth branches, leaves, blossoms, and produces fruits. All these virtues were hidden and potential in the seed. Through the blessing and bounty of cultivation these virtues became apparent. Similarly, the merciful God, our Creator, has deposited within human realities certain latent and*

*potential virtues. Through education and culture these virtues deposited by the loving God will become apparent in the human reality, even as the unfoldment of the tree from within the germinating seed.*—'Abdu'l-Bahá

(*The Promulgation of Universal Peace*, p. 125)

*The greatest bestowal of God to man is the capacity to attain human virtues.*—'Abdu'l-Bahá

(*The Promulgation of Universal Peace*, p. 534)

Couples should strive for a strong commitment to unity based on a mutual submission to the will of God. Such commitment presupposes knowledge of the conditions that maintain unity and the volitional capacity to reflect that knowledge in action:

*The attainment of any object is conditioned upon knowledge, volition and action. Unless these three conditions are forthcoming, there is no execution or accomplishment.*
—'Abdu'l-Bahá
(*Promulgation of Universal Peace*, p. 218)

*Mere knowledge of principles is not sufficient. We all know and admit that justice is good, but there is need of volition and action to carry out and manifest it. . . . All of us know that international peace is good, that it is conducive to human welfare and the glory of man, but volition and action are necessary before it can be established.*—'Abdu'l-Bahá
(*Promulgation of Universal Peace*, pp. 167–68)

Volitional capacity means we have the capability to make a choice or decision and the will to see it carried through. This determination or volitional capacity includes the ability to persevere through tests and difficulties. Without such perseverance, the fortress cannot be built or maintained.

> *Persevere thou in helping His Cause through the strengthening power of the hosts of wisdom and utterance. Thus hath it been decreed by God, the Gracious, the All-Praised. Blessed is the believer who hath in this Day embraced the Truth and the man of fixed resolve whom the hosts of tyranny have been powerless to affright.*—Bahá'u'lláh
>
> (*Tablets of Bahá'u'lláh*, p. 249)

*Perseverance is an essential condition. In every project firmness and steadfastness will undoubtedly lead to good results. . . .*—'Abdu'l-Baha
(*Selections from the Writings of 'Abdu'l-Bahá*, no. 124.1)

*The harder you strive to attain your goal, the greater will be the confirmations of Bahá'u'lláh, and the more certain you can feel to attain success. Be cheerful, therefore, and exert yourself with full faith and confidence.*
—On behalf of Shoghi Effendi
(*The Compilation of Compilations*, 2:1706)

## CONDITIONS THAT MAINTAIN UNITY

Since it is not possible to escape all conflicts or difficulties in married life, marriage partners need to have a good understanding of how unity can be maintained in spite of these tests. The basic conditions that maintain unity are those that enable a married couple to handle tests successfully, while also sustaining a spiritual vision of marriage. A basic acceptance of our purpose in life, knowing and loving God, is prerequisite to the establishment of these conditions.

> *Know that this unity cannot be maintained save through faith in the Covenant of God.*—'Abdu'l-Bahá
> (*Selections from the Writings of 'Abdu'l-Bahá*, no. 186.7)

> *Our Heavenly Father will always give us the strength to meet and overcome tests if we turn with all our*

*hearts to Him, and difficulties if they are met in the right spirit only make us rely on God more firmly and completely.*

—On behalf of Shoghi Effendi

(*Lights of Guidance*, no. 1378)

*It is one of the essential teachings of the Faith that unity should be maintained in the home. Of course this does not mean that any member of the family has a right to influence the faith of any other member; and if this is realized by all the members, then it seems certain that unity would be feasible.*

—On behalf of Shoghi Effendi

(*The Compilation of Compilations*, 1:896)

If these conditions are missing, both must set about to create them by studying Bahá'u'lláh's writings and by praying and meditating. As knowing and loving God become a part of oneself, knowing and loving others are inevitable consequences. Such knowing and loving fulfill our purpose, give meaning to our lives that will sustain a spiritual view of marriage, and provide the fundamental conditions for handling all other tests and difficulties successfully.

When tensions or conflicts do arise, they must be identified and discussed with both frankness and love. Open communication and frequent consultation are essential to the maintenance of unity within a marriage.

> *In all things it is necessary to consult. . . . inasmuch as it is and will always be a cause of awareness and of awakening and a source of good and well-being.*—Bahá'u'lláh
>
> (*The Compilation of Compilations,* 1:170)

*Consultation bestoweth greater awareness and transmuteth conjecture into certitude. It is a shining light which, in a dark world, leadeth the way and guideth. For everything there is and will continue to be a station of perfection and maturity. The maturity of the gift of understanding is made manifest through consultation.*
—Bahá'u'lláh

(*The Compilation of Compilations,* 1:168)

*Settle all things, both great and small, by consultation. Without prior consultation, take no important step in your own personal affairs. Concern yourselves with one another. Help along one another's projects and plans. Grieve over one another.*
. . . —'Abdu'l-Bahá

(*Lights of Guidance,* no. 588)

*Consultation must have for its object the investigation of truth. He who expresses an opinion should not voice it as correct and right but set it forth as a contribution to the consensus of opinion, for the light of reality becomes apparent when two opinions coincide. A spark is produced when flint and steel come together. Man should weigh his opinions with the utmost serenity, calmness and composure. Before expressing his own views he should carefully consider the views already advanced by others. If he finds that a previously expressed opinion is more true and worthy, he should accept it immediately and not willfully hold to an opinion of his own. By this excellent method he endeavors to arrive at unity and truth.*—'Abdu'l-Bahá

(*The Promulgation of Universal Peace,* pp. 99–100)

*The purpose of consultation is to show that the views of several individuals are assuredly preferable to one man, even as the power of a number of men is of course greater than the power of one man. Thus consultation is acceptable in the presence of the Almighty, and hath been enjoined upon the believers, so that they may confer upon ordinary and personal matters, as well as on affairs which are general in nature and universal.*—'Abdu'l-Bahá

(*Lights of Guidance*, no. 580)

*Bahá'u'lláh came to bring unity to the world, and a fundamental unity is that of the family. Therefore, one must believe that the Faith is intended to strengthen the family, not weaken it, and one of the keys to the*

*strengthening of unity is loving consultation.*

—The Universal House of Justice

(*Lights of Guidance*, no. 734)

Frank consultation is frequently misunderstood to be a process that can undermine unity rather than sustain it. Knowledge of possible misunderstandings about the purpose and spirit of consultation and how they can affect the marital relationship may help prevent them or prove useful in dealing with them when they do appear.

1. Frank consultation is not aggressive confrontation. Whenever consultation is used as a means of expressing hostility, perversity, or rancor, its purpose—which is to find the truth of the situation so action can be taken—is thwarted. Furthermore, using consul-

tation for giving vent to such negative emotions creates hurt feelings and mistrust that must then be overcome. These are the inevitable consequences of relating to another person in an unspiritual way. One's relationship to another person during consultation is unspiritual if his motives are impure or inconsistent with the fundamental purpose of the consultation, which is to restore unity by resolving conflicts.

> *O ye beloved of the Lord! Commit not that which defileth the limpid stream of love or destroyeth the sweet fragrance of friendship. By the righteousness of the Lord! Ye were created to show love one to another and not perversity and rancor. Take pride not in love for yourselves but in love for your fellow-creatures.*—Bahá'u'lláh
>
> (*Tablets of Bahá'u'lláh*, p. 138)

*Conflict and contention are categorically forbidden in His Book. This is a decree of God in this Most Great Revelation.*—Bahá'u'lláh

(*Tablets of Bahá'u'lláh,* p. 221)

*Consultation has been ordained by Bahá'u'lláh as the means by which agreement is to be reached and a collective course of action defined. It is applicable to the marriage partners and within the family, and indeed in all areas where believers participate in mutual decision-making. It requires all participants to express their opinions with absolute freedom and without apprehension that they will be censured and/or their views belittled. . . .*

—The Universal House of Justice

(In a letter written January 24, 1993)

2. Consultation is not a means for fixing blame, since doing so undermines its basic purpose. Usually a rehearsal of who did what is unnecessary, since these facts are already known.

> *It behooveth you, therefore, to attach blame to no one except to yourselves, for the things ye have committed, if ye but judge fairly.*—Bahá'u'lláh
>
> (*Gleanings from the Writings of Bahá'u'lláh*, no. 113.8)

> *So far as ye are able, ignite a candle of love in every meeting, and with tenderness rejoice and cheer ye every heart. Care for the stranger as for one of your own; show to alien souls the same loving kindness ye bestow upon your faithful friends. Should any come to blows with you, seek*

*to be friends with him; should any stab you to the heart, be ye a healing salve unto his sores; should any taunt and mock at you, meet him with love. Should any heap his blame upon you, praise ye him; should he offer you a deadly poison, give him the choicest honey in exchange; and should he threaten your life, grant him a remedy that will heal him evermore. Should he be pain itself, be ye his medicine; should he be thorns, be ye his roses and sweet herbs. Perchance such ways and words from you will make this darksome world turn bright at last; will make this dusty earth turn heavenly, this devilish prison place become a royal palace of the Lord—so that war and strife will pass and be no more, and love and trust will pitch their tents on the summits of the world. Such is the essence of God's admonitions; such in sum are the teachings for the Dispensation of Bahá.*

—'Abdu'l-Bahá

(*Selections from the Writings of 'Abdu'l-Bahá*, no. 16.5)

A more important task during consultation is determining the reasons for what caused the difficulty.

3. Consultation is not a forum for nagging. Consultation is a way for the involved parties to speak openly about issues that need to be resolved, but it should not be looked at simply as an opportunity to vent hurt feelings or focus on what we feel others did or are doing wrong.

*Do not complain of others. Refrain from reprimanding them, and if you*

*wish to give admonition or advice, let it be offered in such a way that it will not burden the bearer.*
—'Abdu'l-Bahá

(*The Promulgation of Universal Peace*, p. 639)

*The members . . . must take counsel together in such wise that no occasion for ill-feeling or discord may arise. This can be attained when every member expresseth with absolute freedom his own opinion and setteth forth his argument. Should any one oppose, he must on no account feel hurt for not until matters are fully discussed can the right way be revealed. The shining spark of truth cometh forth only after the clash of differing opinions.*—'Abdu'l-Bahá

(Quoted in *Bahá'í Administration*, p. 21)

Nagging fails to solve the existing problems, and it creates new ones. Nagging or speaking to others in a condescending tone robs one of energy and greatly reduces the inclination, on the part of the person who is being nagged or spoken to in a negative or hurtful way, to communicate. When communication ceases or becomes concerned only with routine matters, it is difficult to analyze, reflect on, and discuss the marriage relationship in order to solve problems.

4. Consultation should not be used as a substitute for action or a temporary catharsis. Although relief from tension may be one beneficial byproduct of consultation, if it does no more than this, it will not foster the growth of the marriage as fully as it might. Consultation should be used to clarify a situation, reestablish the basis for unity, resolve

conflicts, and make decisions for action that will help to prevent future difficulties arising from the same issues.

Consultation is not only problem solving and reaching decisions in regard to difficulties being faced. It is also the means of exchanging and communicating aspirations, lofty ideals, encouragement, and loving support so that the marriage partners may *"improve the spiritual life of each other."** If more time were spent engaging in this kind of consultation, less time would be needed for consultation related to problem solving and the resolution of conflicts.

---

* 'Abdu'l-Bahá, in *Selections from the Writings of 'Abdu'l-Bahá,* no. 86.2.

## IMMATURITY AND MAINTAINING UNITY

In many marriages, the most difficult situations to resolve occur because one of the marriage partners is less mature than the other. Inevitably, such an imbalance makes it difficult to maintain unity and a smoothly functioning home. The less mature partner may frequently manifest selfishness, jealousy, lack of responsibility, unreasonable expectations of being waited on, unreasonable demands, mismanagement of money and other family resources, and, most difficult of all, a persistent inability to admit these immaturities and thereby begin to work on them. A marriage partner struggling with these immaturities will be likely to respond negatively to "consultation" that is used to find fault, place blame, or nag. On the contrary, the other partner needs to develop patience, courtesy, slowness to anger, purity of motive, and selflessness in order to help facilitate the spiritual growth of the one whose immaturities are a source of tests and difficulties. This places a heavy responsibility on both, but the more mature partner may have to take the initiative to spiritualize the union and help facilitate the growth toward maturity.

> *A kindly tongue is the lodestone of the hearts of men. It is the bread of the spirit, it clotheth the words with meaning, it is the fountain of the light of wisdom and understanding.*
> —Bahá'u'lláh
>
> (*Gleanings from the Writings of Bahá'u'lláh*, no. 132.5)

> *Blessed are they who hold fast to the rope of compassion and kindness*

*and are detached from animosity and hatred!*
—Bahá'u'lláh

(*Tablets of Bahá'u'lláh*, p. 36)

*Well is it with him who is illumined with the light of courtesy and is attired with the vesture of uprightness. Whoso is endued with courtesy hath indeed attained a sublime station.*
—Bahá'u'lláh

(*Tablets of Bahá'u'lláh*, p. 88)

*Be in perfect unity. Never become angry with one another. . . . Love the creatures for the sake of God and not for themselves. You will never become angry or impatient if you love them for the sake of God.*—'Abdu'l-Bahá

(*The Promulgation of Universal Peace*, p. 128)

*We can never exert the influence over others which we can exert over ourselves. If we are better, if we show love, patience, and understanding of the weakness of others, if we seek to never criticize but rather encourage, others will do likewise. . . .*
—Shoghi Effendi
(*Lights of Guidance*, no. 291)

**SPIRITUALIZING THE UNION**

Bahá'u'lláh said that He made marriage not only a *"fortress for well-being"* but a fortress of *"salvation"* as well. Bahá'u'lláh's appearance is the source of our salvation for He has come to teach us the purpose of our lives, thereby putting us in touch with reality.

*If all should be true to the original reality of the Prophet and His teach-*

*ing, the peoples and nations of the world would become unified, and these differences which cause separation would be lost sight of.*
—'Abdu'l-Bahá

(*The Promulgation of Universal Peace*, p. 446)

*Verily, God has chosen you for His love and knowledge; God has chosen you for the worthy service of unifying mankind; God has chosen you for the purpose of investigating reality and promulgating international peace; God has chosen you for the progress and development of humanity, for spreading and proclaiming true education, for the expression of love toward your fellow creatures and the removal of prejudice; God has chosen you to blend together human hearts*

*and give light to the human world. The doors of His generosity are wide, wide open to us; but we must be attentive, alert and mindful, occupied with service to all mankind, appreciating the bestowals of God and ever conforming to His will.*
—'Abdu'l-Bahá

(*The Promulgation of Universal Peace*, p. 474)

Salvation from a Bahá'í point of view means release from material bondage. Marriage as a fortress for salvation therefore depends upon a spiritual foundation that is wholly consistent with the reality of men and women as spiritual beings. While Bahá'í marriage means both spiritual and physical union, 'Abdu'l-Bahá makes it clear that the union cannot endure without a spiritual basis.

*The Lord, peerless is He, hath made woman and man to abide with each other in the closest companionship, and to be even as a single soul. They are two helpmates, two intimate friends, who should be concerned about the welfare of each other.*

*If they live thus, they will pass through this world with perfect contentment, bliss, and peace of heart, and become the object of divine grace and favor in the Kingdom of heaven.*—'Abdu'l-Bahá

(*Selections from the Writings of 'Abdu'l-Bahá*, no. 92.1–2)

## THE ROLE OF PRAYER AND STUDYING THE WRITINGS IN PRESERVING A MARRIAGE

The kinds of difficulties that come to a marriage because of the immaturities of the marriage partners themselves can only be handled successfully by spiritual means. Ultimately, each of these difficulties is caused by an absence of one or more of those virtues, or attributes of God, that 'Abdu'l-Bahá says it is the purpose of our lives to acquire. Studying the writings and praying are the door to the acquisition of these virtues.

> *Such hindrances . . . no matter how severe and insuperable they may at first seem, can and should be effectively overcome through the combined and sustained power of prayer and of determined and continued effort.*
>
> —On behalf of Shoghi Effendi
>
> (Quoted in letter written on behalf of the Universal House of Justice, *Lights of Guidance*, no. 955)

Those who are having marital difficulties must realize that, if they are sincere in their desire to resolve these difficulties, their attitude must include humility and fear of God, both of which enable prayer and daily exposure to Bahá'u'lláh's word to have their greatest effect.

> *O SON OF MAN!*
> *Humble thyself before Me, that I may graciously visit thee.*—Bahá'u'lláh
>
> (The Hidden Words, Arabic, no. 42)

> *The fear of God hath ever been the prime factor in the education of His creatures. Well is it with them that have attained thereunto!*
> —Bahá'u'lláh
>
> (*Epistle to the Son of the Wolf*, p. 27)

[Divine Knowledge] *welleth out from the fountain of divine inspiration. . . .* [Its] *source . . . is God Himself. . . .* [It] *is guided by the principle: "Fear ye God; God will teach you" . . . .*
—Bahá'u'lláh

(The Kitáb-i-Íqán, ¶76)

*Our part it is to act in accordance with the teaching of Bahá'u'lláh in humility and firm steadfastness.*
—'Abdu'l-Bahá

(*Paris Talks*, no. 33.25)

*Let your thoughts dwell on your own spiritual development, and close your eyes to the deficiencies of other souls. Act ye in such wise, showing forth pure and goodly deeds, and modesty and humility, that ye will cause others to be awakened.*—'Abdu'l-Bahá

(*Selections from the Writings of 'Abdu'l-Bahá*, no. 174.5)

Immaturities often involve an egocentric perspective on life and personal relationships. Any perspective that is egocentric is necessarily incomplete and therefore an inadequate view of the reality of any given situation. Responses based on such a view will almost always be selfish.

*Through the assistance and providence of God and through the bounties of the Kingdom of Abha you may be entirely severed from the imperfections of the world of nature, purified from selfish, human desires, receiving life from the Kingdom*

*of Abha and attaining heavenly graces.*—'Abdu'l-Bahá

(*The Promulgation of Universal Peace*, p. 452)

*Bahá'u'lláh endured the greatest hardships. He found neither rest by night nor peace by day. He was constantly under the stress of great calamity—now in prison, now in chains, now threatened by the sword—until finally He broke the cage of captivity, left this mortal world and ascended to the heaven of God. He endured all these tribulations for our sakes and suffered these deprivations that we might attain the bestowals of divine bounty. Therefore, we must be faithful to Him and turn away from our own selfish desires and fancies in order*

*that we may accomplish that which is required of us by our Lord.*
—'Abdu'l-Bahá

(*The Promulgation of Universal Peace*, p. 651)

Although working through one marriage partner's immaturities may feel difficult at times, they are not impossible to overcome, especially when the couple chooses to rely on spiritual means to solve the problems.

*There are . . . innumerable examples of individuals who have been able to effect drastic and enduring changes in their behavior, through drawing on the spiritual powers available by the bounty of God.*
—On behalf of the Universal House of Justice

(*The Compilation of Compilations*, 2:2347)

Responses that are selfish inhibit the growth of interpersonal relationships and ultimately lead to estrangement. Among the most frequent difficulties marriage partners face is trying to overcome estrangement that has arisen out of selfishness, lack of restraint, and saying things that are not meant but are nevertheless hurtful and damaging. Consultation entered in a state of estrangement will usually be unsuccessful. For this reason consultation should be undertaken after prayer has removed the estrangement.

> *Shut your eyes to estrangement, then fix your gaze upon unity. Cleave tenaciously unto that which will lead to the well-being and tranquillity of all mankind.*—Bahá'u'lláh
>
> (*Tablets of Bahá'u'lláh*, p. 67)

> *Souls are inclined toward estrangement. Steps should first be taken to do away with this estrangement, for only then will the Word take effect.*—'Abdu'l-Bahá
>
> (*Selections from the Writings of 'Abdu'l-Bahá*, no. 209.3)

One of the basic functions of prayer is to alter an egocentric perspective into a selfless, or spiritual, perspective. Once someone's perspective has been changed, their feelings will be altered, and the way can then be paved for finding a solution in mutually supportive ways.

Prayer also has the effects of inclining one to be protective of the marital union and helping to obviate a need for discussing private matters with others outside the marriage. Indiscriminate discussion of marital concerns is likely to undermine steadfastness and perseverance, which are among the important requisites to a good marriage.

— 11 —

# Seeking Assistance from the Spiritual Assembly

In some instances, even after much sincere effort and perseverance with an attitude of humility, the marriage situation continues to worsen. The married couple may then require assistance from the Local Spiritual Assembly. This Bahá'í institution has been endowed with the capacity to bring to bear its collective wisdom on a given problem through consultation, by clarifying issues, sifting fact from speculation, and identifying spiritual principles that need to be applied in solving problems. The Local Spiritual Assembly will in all likelihood be able to suggest a number of alternatives that can then be tried out for a period of time, after which the Local Assembly may wish to reassess the situation and provide additional assistance.

> *If, God forbid, they* [husband and wife] *fail to agree, and their disagreement leads to estrangement, they should seek counsel from those they trust and in whose sincerity and sound judgment they have confidence, in order to preserve and strengthen their ties as a united family.*
> —On behalf of the Universal House of Justice
> (*Compilations of Compilations*, 2:2341)

If sincere efforts to build a sound marriage do not prove fruitful, it may be undesirable and even harmful for the husband and wife to remain together. In the Bahá'í Faith, divorce is strongly discouraged. It should be sought as a last resort only in the case of extreme aversion and irreparable disunity, when all other means of reconciliation have failed.

> *The friends (Bahá'ís) must strictly refrain from divorce unless something arises which compels them to separate because of their aversion for each other; in that case, with the knowledge of the Spiritual Assembly, they may decide to separate. They must then be patient and wait one complete year. If during this year harmony is not reestablished between*

*them, then their divorce may be realized. . . . The foundation of the Kingdom of God is based upon harmony and love, oneness, relationship and union, not upon differences, especially between husband and wife. If one of these two become the cause of divorce, that one will unquestionably fall into great difficulties, will become the victim of formidable calamities and experience deep remorse.*—'Abdu'l-Bahá

(Quoted in *Bahá'u'lláh and the New Era*, p. 196)

*There is no doubt about it that the believers in America, probably unconsciously influenced by the extremely lax morals prevalent and the flippant attitude towards divorce which seems to be increasingly pre-*

*vailing, do not take divorce seriously enough and do not seem to grasp the fact that although Bahá'u'lláh has permitted it, He has only permitted it as a last resort and strongly condemns it.*

*The presence of children, as a factor in divorce, cannot be ignored, for surely it places an even greater weight of moral responsibility on the man and wife in considering such a step. Divorce under such circumstances no longer just concerns them and their desires and feelings but also concerns the children's entire future and their own attitude towards marriage.*

—On behalf of Shoghi Effendi

(*The Compilation of Compilations,* 2:2327)

*Wherever there is a Bahá'í family, those concerned should by all means do all they can to preserve it, because divorce is strongly condemned in the Teachings, whereas harmony, unity and love are held up as the highest ideals in human relationships.*

—On behalf of Shoghi Effendi

(*Lights of Guidance*, no. 738)

*Bahá'u'lláh considers the marriage bond very sacred; and only under very exceptional and unbearable circumstances is divorce advisable. . . .*

—On behalf of Shoghi Effendi

(*Lights of Guidance*, no. 1310)

Although divorce is abhorred, Bahá'u'lláh has made provision for it; and if two Bahá'ís seeking divorce proceed according to the principles and spirit of Bahá'í law, no stigma whatever can be attached to them. A couple that has been unable to reconcile their differences should consult with their Local Spiritual Assembly prior to making the decision to divorce.

> *Divorce is conditional upon the approval and permission of the Spiritual Assembly. The members of the Assembly must in such matters independently and carefully study and investigate each case. If there should be valid grounds for divorce and it is found that reconciliation it utterly impossible, that antipathy is intense and its removal is not possible, then the Assembly may approve the divorce.*—Shoghi Effendi
>
> (*Lights of Guidance*, no. 1307)

> *It is necessary that Bahá'ís who intend to divorce be aware that they must consult with their Local or National Assembly that basically a*

> *year of waiting must ensue before divorce can be effected, and that the Assembly has certain responsibilities toward the couple concerned about which they will be informed through consultation with the Assembly.*
>
> —The Universal House of Justice
> (*Lights of Guidance,* no. 1317)

When divorce has been carried out within the spirit of the Faith, the divorced couple are still able to relate to each other in ways that neither hurt each other nor disrupt the unity of the community to which they belong.

> *Love is the standard which must govern the conduct of one believer towards another.*
>
> —On behalf of Shoghi Effendi
> (*Lights of Guidance,* no. 1340)

— 12 —

# Remarriage

After divorce has been effected, remarriage is possible. But a note of caution may be in order. Sometimes there can be such loneliness immediately following divorce that it makes any person one meets seem like a promising spouse. That loneliness is often coupled with the same immaturities that led to marital disunity during the first marriage. Such a combination makes preparation for marriage all the more important, for one who has already had the experience of marriage may think that is has automatically prepared him or her for a second marriage. Allowing enough time for perspective to be gained and adequate preparation for remarriage to take place may be a sound and sensible decision.

All the laws concerning marriage (such as consent of parents and having a Bahá'í ceremony) are binding in the case of remarriage. If all of these laws are observed and the remarriage is contracted with the love of God, it will attract blessings and happiness.

> *Let your hearts be filled with the great love of God, let it be felt by all; for every man is a servant of God, and all are entitled to a share of the Divine Bounty.*—'Abdu'l-Bahá
>
> (*Paris Talks*, no. 5.24)

*The love which exists between the hearts of believers is prompted by the ideal of the unity of spirits. This love is attained through the knowledge of God, so that men see the Divine Love reflected in the heart. Each sees in the other the Beauty of God reflected in the soul, and finding this point of similarity, they are attracted to one another in love. This love will make all men the waves of one sea, this love will make them all the stars of one heaven and the fruits of one tree. This love will bring the realization of true accord, the foundation of real unity.*—'Abdu'l-Bahá

(*Paris Talks*, no. 58.7)

*I charge you all that each one of you concentrate all the thoughts of your heart on love and unity. . . .*

*Thoughts of love are constructive of brotherhood, peace, friendship, and happiness.*—'Abdu'l-Bahá
(*Paris Talks,* no. 6.7–8)

*Know thou of a certainty that Love is the secret of God's holy Dispensation, the manifestation of the All-Merciful, the fountain of spiritual outpourings. Love is heaven's kindly light, the Holy Spirit's eternal breath that vivifieth the human soul. Love is the cause of God's revelation unto man, the vital bond inherent, in accordance with the divine creation, in the realities of things. Love is the one means that ensureth true felicity both in this world and the next. Love is the light that guideth in darkness, the living link that uniteth God with man, that as-*

*sureth the progress of every illumined soul.*

—'Abdu'l-Bahá

(*Selections from the Writings of 'Abdu'l-Bahá*, no. 12.1)

# Conclusion

In order for marriages to become a source of strength, unity, and harmony in our communities and in wider society, a new definition of marriage needs to emerge. Bahá'u'lláh has revealed that marriage has the potential to become "a fortress for well-being and salvation" and has called on humanity to uphold this sacred institution. Although we live in societies that often challenge us in myriad ways because of prevalent lax attitudes and behaviors, especially in regards to the importance of the marriage bond, we will be able to withstand these powerful negative forces by turning to the Word of God and by recognizing the sanctity of this spiritual fortress.

Bahá'í marriage is based on the concept of submission to the will of God, a desire to serve God, a willingness to work and strive to better oneself and draw nearer to God, reliance on consultation as a source of unity within the marriage, and a focus on the spiritual education of children in order to achieve the betterment of the world. Upholding the institution of marriage is a sacred responsibility and is one of the ways we can contribute to the healing of an ailing world.

> *Cleave thou, therefore, with the whole affection of thine heart, unto His love, and withdraw it from the love of any one besides Him, that He may aid thee to immerse thyself in*

*the ocean of His unity, and enable thee to become a true upholder of His oneness.*—Bahá'u'lláh

(*Gleanings from the Writings of Bahá'u'lláh*, no. 114.15)

*Through each and every one of the verses which the Pen of the Most High hath revealed, the doors of love and unity have been unlocked and flung open. . . .*—Bahá'u'lláh

(*Gleanings from the Writings of Bahá'u'lláh*, no. 43.6)

*The more love is expressed among mankind and the stronger the power of unity, the greater will be this reflection and revelation, for the greatest bestowal of God is love.*
—'Abdu'l-Bahá

(*The Promulgation of Universal Peace*, p. 20)

*May you become the quintessence of love. May you prove to be the effulgence of God, replete with the efficacy of the Holy Spirit and the cause of unity and fellowship in the world of humanity, for today mankind has the greatest need of love and agreement.*—'Abdu'l-Bahá

(*The Promulgation of Universal Peace*, p. 455)

# Bibliography

## Works of Bahá'u'lláh

*Epistle to the Son of the Wolf.* Translated by Shoghi Effendi. 1st pocket-sized ed. Wilmette, IL: Bahá'í Publishing Trust, 1988.

*Gleanings from the Writings of Bahá'u'lláh.* Translated by Shoghi Effendi. New ed. Wilmette, IL: Bahá'í Publishing, 2005.

*The Hidden Words of Bahá'u'lláh.* Translated by Shoghi Effendi. Wilmette, IL: Bahá'í Publishing, 2002.

*Kitáb-i-Aqdas: The Most Holy Book.* 1st pocket-sized ed. Wilmette, IL: Bahá'í Publishing Trust, 1993.

*Kitáb-i-Íqán: The Book of Certitude.* Translated by Shoghi Effendi. Wilmette, IL: Bahá'í Publishing, 2003.

*Prayers and Meditations*. Translated by Shoghi Effendi. 1st pocket-sized ed. Wilmette, IL: Bahá'í Publishing Trust, 1987.

*Tablets of Bahá'u'lláh revealed after the Kitáb-i-Aqdas*. Compiled by the Research Department of the Universal House of Justice. Translated by Habib Taherzadeh et al. Wilmette, IL: Bahá'í Publishing Trust, 1988.

### Works of 'Abdu'l-Bahá

*'Abdu'l-Bahá in London: Addresses and Notes of Conversations*. London: Bahá'í Publishing Trust, 1982.

*Paris Talks: Addresses Given by 'Abdu'l-Bahá in Paris in 1911*. Wilmette, IL: Bahá'í Publishing, 2006.

*The Promulgation of Universal Peace: Talks Delivered by 'Abdu'l-Bahá during His Visit to the United States and Canada in 1912*. Compiled by Howard MacNutt. Wilmette, IL: Bahá'í Publishing Trust, 2007.

*The Secret of Divine Civilization.* 1st pocket-size ed. Translated by Marzieh Gail and Ali-Kuli Khan. Wilmette, IL: Bahá'í Publishing Trust, 1990.

*Selections from the Writings of 'Abdu'l-Bahá.* Compiled by the Research Department of the Universal House of Justice. Translated by a Committee at the Bahá'í World Center and by Marzieh Gail. 1st pocket-sized ed. Wilmette, IL: Bahá'í Publishing Trust, 1996.

*Some Answered Questions.* Compiled and translated by Laura Clifford Barney. 1st pocket-sized ed. Wilmette, IL: Bahá'í Publishing Trust, 2004.

**Works of Shoghi Effendi**

*The Advent of Divine Justice.* New ed. Wilmette, IL: Bahá'í Publishing Trust, 2006.

*Bahá'í Administration: Selected Messages, 1922–1932.* 7th ed. Wilmette, IL: Bahá'í Publishing Trust, 1974.

*God Passes By.* Rev. ed. Wilmette, IL: Bahá'í Publishing Trust, 1974.

*Messages to Canada.* 2nd ed. Thornhill, Ont.: Bahá'í Canada Publications, 1999.

*The World Order of Bahá'u'lláh: Selected Letters.* New ed. Wilmette, IL: Bahá'í Publishing Trust, 1991.

## Works of the Universal House of Justice

*Messages from the Universal House of Justice, 1963–1986: The Third Epoch of the Formative Age.* Compiled by Geoffry Marks. Wilmette, IL: Bahá'í Publishing Trust, 1996.

*Messages from the Universal House of Justice, 1968–1973.* Wilmette, IL: Bahá'í Publishing Trust, 1976.

## Compilations from the Bahá'í Writings

*Bahá'í Marriage and Family Life: Selection from the Writings of the Bahá'í Faith.* Originally published by the

National Spiritual Assembly of the Bahá'ís of Canada, 1983. Reprint, Wilmette, IL: Bahá'í Publishing Trust, 1997.

*Bahá'í Prayers: A Selection of Prayers Revealed by Bahá'u'lláh, the Báb, and 'Abdu'l-Bahá.* Wilmette, IL: Bahá'í Publishing Trust, 2002.

*The Compilation of Compilations: Prepared by the Universal House of Justice 1963–1990.* 2 Vols. Australia: Bahá'í Publications Australia, 1991.

*The Divine Art of Living: Selections from the Writings of Bahá'u'lláh, the Báb, and 'Abdu'l-Bahá.* Compiled by Maybel Hyde Paine. Revised by Anne Marie Scheffer. Wilmette, IL: Bahá'í Publishing, 2006.

*Lights of Guidance: A Bahá'í Reference File.* 6th ed. New Dehli, India: Bahá'í Publishing Trust, 1999.

## Other Works

*Developing Distinctive Bahá'í Communities: Guidelines for Spiritual As-*

*semblies*. Evanston, IL: Office of Assembly Development, 2007.

The National Spiritual Assembly of the United States and Canada. "Bahá'í Marriage." *Bahá'í News* 192 (February 1947): 6–7.

The National Spiritual Assembly of the United States. "From the Guardian to the NSA." *Bahá'í News* 236 (October 1950): 2–3.

The National Spiritual Assembly of the United States. "Explanations and Directives Written on Behalf of the Guardian by His Secretary." *Bahá'í News* 283 (September 1954): 1–2.

# Index

## AND THE BAHÁ'Í FAITH

Bahá'í Publishing produces books based on the teachings of the Bahá'í Faith. Founded over 160 years ago, the Bahá'í Faith has spread to some 235 nations and territories and is now accepted by more than five million people. The word "Bahá'í" means "follower of Bahá'u'lláh." Bahá'u'lláh, the founder of the Bahá'í Faith, asserted that He is the Messenger of God for all of humanity in this day. The cornerstone of His teachings is the establishment of the spiritual unity of humankind, which will be achieved by personal transformation and the application of clearly identified spiritual principles. Bahá'ís also believe that there is but one religion and that all the Messengers of God—among them Abraham, Zoroaster, Moses, Krishna, Buddha, Jesus, and Muḥammad—have progressively revealed its nature. Together, the world's great religions are expressions of a single, unfolding divine plan. Human beings, not God's Messengers, are the source of religious divisions, prejudices, and hatreds.

The Bahá'í Faith is not a sect or denomination of another religion, nor is it a cult or a social movement. Rather, it is a globally recognized independent world religion founded on new books of scripture revealed by Bahá'u'lláh.

Bahá'í Publishing is an imprint of the National Spiritual Assembly of the Bahá'ís of the United States.

For more information about the Bahá'í Faith,<br>or to contact Bahá'ís near you, visit<br>http://www.bahai.us/<br>or call 1-800-22-UNITE

## Other Books Available from Bahá'í Publishing

**HERITAGE OF LIGHT**
The Spiritual Destiny of America
Janet A. Khan
$17.00 US / $19.00 CAN
Trade Paper
ISBN 978-1-931847-73-5

*An examination of a fascinating religious community and a penetrating look at the spiritual destiny of America*

*Heritage of Light* is an accessible description of the American Bahá'í community and a penetrating look at the spiritual destiny of America. This exploration traces the historical and spiritual connections that link the American Bahá'ís with the early Bahá'ís of Iran, who displayed an unparalleled staunchness of faith and heroism in the face of unspeakable brutal persecution and oppression. The author's examination of the writings of the Bahá'í Faith, along with extensive historical and archival records, demonstrates the unique role assigned to the American Bahá'ís and to the American nation as a whole in the development of a unified global society and the eventual inauguration of a world civilization.

**ILLUMINE MY WORLD**

Bahá'í Prayers and Meditations for Peace
Bahá'u'lláh, the Báb, and 'Abdu'l-Bahá
$14.00 US / $16.00 CAN
Trade Paper
ISBN 978-1-931847-65-0

*A heartwarming collection of prayers designed for people of all faiths during times of anxiety and chaos in the world*

*Illumine My World* is a collection of prayers and meditative passages from the writings of the

Bahá'í Faith that will help bring comfort and assurance during a time of growing anxiety, chaos, and change in the world today. As financial and religious institutions crumble and fall, as the tide of refugees from countries torn by civil strife continues to grow, as the oppression of women and minorities are brought to light more and more in so many parts of the world, readers can take comfort from these soothing passages. The prayers included specifically ask, among other things, for protection, for unity, and for assistance from God. Individuals from all religions will find strength and assurance in this inspiring collection.

**UNDERSTANDING DEATH**

The Most Important Event of Your Life

John S. Hatcher

$18.00 US / $20.00 CAN

Trade Paper

ISBN 978-1-931847-72-8

*A personal exploration of mortality and death, the inevitable journey of human life, and the acceptance of faith*

*Understanding Death: The Most Important Event of Your Life* illustrates the need to prepare for this important moment, even though many ignore its inevitability. There is no escape from death and the grief that can consume one when faced by the loss of family and friends. The author's personal insight offers encouragement that death is not the end but the beginning of a new spiritual existence. Author John Hatcher surveys his own life, the decisions he has made over the years, and how those experiences have impacted him. He especially focuses on his discovery and exploration of the Bahá'í Faith and his eventual acceptance of Bahá'u'lláh's teachings. Accepting that death is not the end, that there is another journey, and that there is time to accept the inevitable and prepare for the life hereafter can bring peace and comfort to all.

**MIND, HEART, & SPIRIT**
Educators Speak
Heather Cardin
$18.00 US / $20.00 CAN
Trade Paper
ISBN 978-1-931847-66-7

*Real-life stories from teachers who share their passion for shaping the lives of young people today*

*Mind, Heart, and Spirit: Educators Speak* is a collection of real-life stories from a diverse group of educators on a wide range of issues such as how to deal with difficult students, the role of parents and religion in a child's education, and the similarities and differences in educating children in different cultures across the globe. Filled with interesting anecdotes and personal accounts, this is an intimate, sometimes frustrating, sometimes exhilarating insight into the experiences of all these educators as they have struggled to overcome various challenges in educating children. Their passion for teaching and their devotion to their students come shining through and offer a glimpse of the important role that Bahá'í education—with its emphasis on unity, tolerance, and diversity—can play in shaping the lives of young people today.